Rose,

What an Honor
to Meet you, and
becoming a part of
Our Ministry.
Blessings ALL Over
you & your family
Joanne Renucci

NEW!

New Thoughts, New Heart, New Life

JOANNE APRIL RANUCCI

You may contact the author, JoAnne April Ranucci, at the following email address: Joanneranucci7@gmail.com

Individuals and church groups may order books from JoAnne April Ranucci directly, or from the publisher. Retailers and wholesalers should order from our distributors. Refer to the Deeper Revelation Books website for distribution information, as well as an online catalog of all our books.

Cover design and Layout: Michael McDonald
www.artfxdesigns.com
artfx2@gmail.com

Published by:
Deeper Revelation Books
Revealing "the deep things of God" (1 Cor. 2:10)
P.O. Box 4260 Cleveland, TN 37320 423-478-2843
Website: *www.deeperrevelationbooks.org*
Email: *info@deeperrevelationbooks.org*

Deeper Revelation Books assists Christian authors in publishing and distributing their books. Final responsibility for design, content, permissions, editorial accuracy, and doctrinal views, either expressed or implied, belongs to the author.

TABLE OF CONTENTS

ILLUSTRATIONS

Except for the butterflies and moths, the illustrations found throughout this book were hand-drawn by the author during various stages of her recovery, so they provide a visual picture of what God was doing in her heart and life.

DEDICATIONS

First and foremost, I dedicate this book to God Almighty. He showed me grace and favor and never gave up on me, even when I gave up on myself. He heard my prayers through my brokenness and lifted me out of my shame.

God laid it on my heart to write this book and I was obedient. The Holy Spirit inspired me to show others that they, too, can rise above the ashes of their lives and be made whole, complete, loved, forgiven, and most of all, saved. I'm very grateful God put this on my heart. I'm forever a child of God.

I also dedicate this book to my parents, Lawrence and Josephine Ranucci, who tried anything and everything to love and help me. At that time I was beyond help, and they lost me through my addictions. They feared for me and cried, never believing I could ever be complete or happy. They feared they had lost me forever. So I dedicate this book to them, to say I've been found, saved, and blessed beyond my wildest dreams. Mom, you can rest easy now, looking down from heaven. You can finally rejoice in what God has done in me. And Dad, you're an eyewitness. See, the prodigal child has come home at last. I love you, Daddy.

To my children, April, Christopher, Brandy, and Nicole, I love you very much. I know, due to my poor choices and addictions, you have all paid a price. I can never begin to understand what each one of you have gone through. I am sorry. I know that we are still working out the pain from our past and the kidnapping. I am, however, grateful that we found each other again, and we have begun to heal. My prayer is, as you read this book, that we will come to find more healing and a greater love for one another.

I also dedicate this book to the family I made for fifteen years in the homeless camps. All of them but a few have passed away because of addiction. A few survive, like my adopted "sister" Pam. My prayers for those who remain is to also find God. We have been through so much, but it's time to come out of the cave of addiction. We need to glorify God and find His peace, love, and joy.

ACKNOWLEDGEMENTS

Mrs. Karilyn Tap, thank you for believing in me and supporting me on this adventure.

Liz McDonald, thank you for encouraging me.

To all those on The Hope Team, thank you for leading me in the right direction and never giving up on me.

And to David Carl, thank you for being in my life and coming to the Lord. Thank you for letting me witness the miracle before my very eyes of seeing your wings spread and becoming a full-blown Christian. It was due to nothing else but the power of forgiveness for this to be possible.

Therefore, if anyone is in Christ,
he is a new creature;
the old things passed away;
behold, new things have come.
(2 Corinthians 5:17)

FOREWORD
From Caterpillar to Butterfly

I always knew something was missing. Even though I had a loving family, I had a "hole." I didn't know it was my "God hole." Everybody has a space only God can fill. Like many other people, I looked to fill this hole with everything else in the world except God.

Now at age 56, I'm looking back. I look at all the destruction I created for all those years. It's like a war zone, worse than a tornado. Two abortions, two adoptions, three abandoned children, four husbands, felonies, prison, estranged relationships with family…I didn't make it to Mom's deathbed to say goodbye before she died. I was told not to attend the funeral because of bad blood between my oldest sister and me.

While I was in jail for a week, my disabled husband died in the hospital of a brain aneurysm. When I came home, I learned that he was dead and that my remaining two children had been taken by strangers while I was in jail – strangers who didn't care about them, just their father's Social Security disability check. These two children later turned to drugs themselves, thinking they weren't worthy of love.

Now with the only two children I had left kidnapped, and the police not taking me seriously because I was an addict, I totally gave up. I became homeless and lived in the woods for the next fifteen years. I stayed numb, drinking every second I was awake and smoking crack so as not to fall asleep. I worked as a prostitute during this time. I don't know how many times I really "should have" died during this period.

I always loved God, and during my times of sobriety, I went to church and joined Bible studies. I even reached out to God during my drug and alcohol-induced periods. I drove myself to church one time so high I just sat in the pew and wrote poems to God. I placed one of them in this book entitled "Please Bring Me Back." I was reaching out to God because all the things that I had thought made me feel good, whole, connected, loved, etc., were just complete lies.

However, I didn't have the right people around me, and I had destroyed many of the good things in my life. The guilt, shame, and hopelessness dragged me down. I needed to believe these lies because they were all I had, even though many of my friends were dying all around me from drug overdoses, alcohol poisoning, walking in front of cars, hanging themselves, getting shot in the back, liver failure or cirrhosis, and on and on.

I would not be here today if it were not for a certain angel of God, Nancy Martinez from The Hope Team, who, along with the rest of The Hope Team, NEVER gave up on me. This is God's honest truth. This is where the change first started.

Then I entered rehab, which became my cocoon for six months. After all the searching through the years of my life, the Bible study there watered seeds planted years before. In rehab, I blossomed! I wasn't a wormy caterpillar anymore - I finally grew my butterfly wings. I changed and became a new creature. God's Holy Spirit ignited a flame that consumed my soul. Now I'll never be the same. I will never go back to being that lost, scared, empty person.

My heart's "hole" is not only filled, but my heart overflows with so much love, joy, peace, and understanding that I have to give it to others. It's an endless flowing gift that runs through my fingers, something I can't hold onto or hoard only for myself. Once you're filled with the Spirit of God, there's no stopping it. It overwhelms and consumes you.

Every aspect of your life now becomes His aspect. You can't help yourself – you want to live through His eyes and His heart and His love. The crazy thing (for me at least) is the more I give it away, the faster I keep filling up with more of His characteristics. Remember I said in the beginning that I felt something was missing. Well, now I've found that something! Knowing who you truly are in Christ, a child of God, is the most important, extreme miracle of a feeling I've ever experienced. Everything makes sense now.

The people who knew me and how I lived before (my family members, my friends, even The Hope Team) are in a state of shock about who I have become. I quit drugs and I quit drinking. The only reason is GOD. I've pruned my life, cutting off all the things that hindered me from growing into my rightful place, the place where I belonged.

Now nothing can ever separate me from the love of God. Romans 8:38-39 says, "For I am convinced that neither death, nor life, nor angels, nor principalities, nor things present, nor things to come, nor powers, nor height, nor depth, nor any other created thing, will be able to separate us from the love of God, which is in Christ Jesus our Lord."

My purpose in writing this book is to let people know that no matter how horrible your circumstances, it's not too late to come to God and apply His Word to your life. God is The Answer to it all. Finding Him is the only way to become a whole person, knowing you are never alone - you are loved, not abandoned. By following Him you will gain a complete life. Not only can you make sense of things, but you will also receive peace, love, and joy that weren't there before. You never again have to be without them!

CHAPTER 1

BUILDING A STRONG FOUNDATION

PART 1 – POURING IN JESUS

When you hear God's words and apply them to your life, you will demonstrate wisdom and your life will benefit. When you follow God's ways, you are building a strong foundation that is secure and won't be destroyed.

"Therefore everyone who hears these words of Mine and acts on them, may be compared to a wise man who built his house on the rock" (Matthew 7:24).

To build a very strong foundation, to build upon a new, clean slate, the old one has to be torn down to its very bottom. The material you pick to build your new foundation has to be the very best. Where you obtain this material is very important since it will define the entire structure and ensure it will stand through all the tests of time.

THE BIBLE IS THIS STRONG FOUNDATION.

I'm going to use my personal experiences and growth to show you how giving birth to new thoughts led me in directions and to accomplishments I never dreamt I would experience.

Knowing your own mind isn't as easy as you think. There are so many distractions and influences. Sometimes it's just plain impossible to know what is really right. Dad taught me the pro-and-con list – "just weigh it out." You have probably heard of this technique.

We can sometimes waste our time and money on various kinds of therapy or even seek to heal our loneliness through avenues such as bars or prostitutes. Knowing the God of the Bible is a much better way to fulfill the void that each of us has from birth.

I have now learned that people cannot find themselves unless they know who created them – the Original Father. Once we know who we are in Christ, then and only then can we walk in the right state of mind, in the light of His truth.

Our minds and our thoughts become darkened from absorbing the world's point of view. The world actually dictates to us the way we should believe and think. The Bible tells us that in Isaiah 55:8: "For my thoughts are not your thoughts, neither are your ways my ways, declares the LORD."

Knowing and having control over our own minds are what we should desire. Giving birth to new thoughts is not instantaneous. It is like a pregnancy. We have to plant the seed and deliberately encourage it to grow. The seed is God's Word, the Bible. Just as we all started from a seed which originated with God, we must develop our minds now in the ways of God. As we nourish our bodies with food, we must now nourish our minds with truth.

God's Word is alive. Once it dwells in us and we start learning His ways, we begin a new way of thinking. Life starts to change for the better once our thoughts begin to conform more and more to God's thoughts. When we learn God's traits and values, we start to acquire integrity and humility.

I'm going to jump ahead for a moment. When we have become mature mentally in the ways of God, we can look back on our former life. That's when I saw all the wrong decisions, friends, and influences that caused me to have the life I had – BAD.

Let's start at the beginning so we can give birth to new thoughts. Once this happens, it's as if our brains burst! Our lives are now meaningful, and new thought patterns will be cultivated. To begin, we must replace the old thoughts and patterns with God's truth. We must start to build our relationship with God. This involves breaking bad habits.

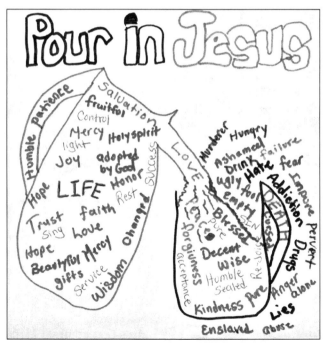

The more you pour Jesus into your life, eventually you start becoming the image of God yourself, and others will see God's light through your life.

The more I learned God's Word, the more I began to experience new feelings, and new thoughts started to form… and finally, new habits. I wasn't alone on this journey. God's Holy Spirit, called "The Comforter," also comes alive in us. The Spirit helps chip away bit by bit the things that hinder true growth. To find the right state of mind, we have to begin with the Truth. God's Word is the Truth.

The mind feeds off of many "gateways," absorbing from everything we touch, see, smell, hear, and taste. Think about spring cleaning. When you start to think God's thoughts, you clean out and clear away all the cobwebs and dust of confusion. You can now see clearly out the windows of your mind, instead of bumping into the clutter of the world's distractions. It's as if you have new, fresh surroundings that don't seem so "doom and gloom."

Until we replace our old thoughts with God's thoughts, we will continue to have hardened hearts. Ephesians 4:18 describes this as "being darkened in their understanding, excluded from the life of God because of the ignorance that is in them, because of the hardness of their heart." We are not going to be fully happy until we get to the place where we belong.

People become addicts for many different reasons. No one is the same. Not only do we become victims of addiction, but our minds become prisoners of all types of evil, conformed to Satan's will. Most addicts have been fed lies (false beliefs) for a long time. It seems impossible to ever get out of the devil's trap.

Even if we do overcome the addiction, our minds are still infected and poisoned. And that part is just as difficult to overcome as the physical addiction! At that point, our minds are so far gone that we're just as mixed up and confused as if we're still addicted.

PART 2 - JUMP IN WITH BOTH FEET

"Therefore, if anyone is in Christ, he is a new creature; the old things passed away; behold, new things have come" (2 Corinthians 5:17).

"And do not be conformed to this world, but be transformed by the renewing of your mind, so that you may prove what the will of God is, that which is good and acceptable and perfect" (Romans 12:2).

"But a natural man does not accept the things of the Spirit of God, for they are foolishness to him; and he cannot understand them, because they are spiritually appraised" (1 Corinthians 2:14).

During a baptismal ceremony, a person gets submerged in water. The person then arising out of the water is a symbol of rebirth. This is the first step – where it all begins. Even though we don't remain physically submerged in water, we must now begin taking the necessary steps to stay "spiritually submerged."

We must maintain our connection constantly and persistently to remain "alive to God in Christ." (Romans 6:11 – "Even so, consider yourselves to be dead to sin, but alive to God in Christ Jesus.") We must give God the highest priority in our lives from here on out. We must always honor our God. He needs to come first in our thoughts.

Our overall wellness depends upon this. When we are right with God, it trickles down into every aspect of our lives. Eventually, we can reach out to others for their benefit.

"All Scripture is inspired by God and profitable for teaching, for reproof, for correction, for training in righteousness; so that the man of God may be adequate, equipped for every good work" (2 Timothy 3:16-17).

As I alluded to earlier, the umbilical cord of God's Word will feed us appropriately with all the spiritual nutrients we need to stay aligned with God.

"I will give them a heart to know Me, for I am the LORD; and they will be My people, and I will be their God, for they will return to Me with their whole heart" (Jeremiah 24:7).

I personally fell in love with God after being an addict for forty years. I was homeless for fifteen of those years and did everything under the sun to find happiness and contentment to fill the loneliness and hopelessness I felt.

Now I'm saved. I invited God into my heart, soul, and life. I look back now and realize WOW! He was there all that time to fulfill my needs. I wasted much of my life looking for something I already possessed – God's love. I just didn't access it.

I am now filled with everything I was lacking. I'll never go back. And if I can be filled, anyone can. To some, it may sound like work; to others, a life-changing event. They're both right! We get out what we put in.

The secret is that the love, respect, and honor we now feel outweighs our selfishness and self-serving attitude. We come to a place where we never want to be without God again. We understand that the root of our joy, peace, and well-being is in that safe place with God.

We become so rooted that even when life happens and we start to drift back into the madness of this corrupt world, God Himself helps us return quickly. And with gladness we do! Like everyone, I have my "off days," but the more I submerge myself in God on my "good days," the more I will be able to reap what I've sown when I need it. Galatians 6:7 says, "For whatever a man sows, this he will also reap."

It is so wonderful to know that God is always consistent, always the same. Hebrews 13:8 says, "Jesus Christ is the same yesterday and today and forever." The strongest of Christians (even pastors and ministry leaders) all become distracted or negatively impacted by life's circumstances from time to time. That's okay because now we have God to help us ride out all the storms. They don't have to turn into monsoons, like they did before we became His children.

As humans living in the flesh, we are capable of reacting to circumstances and problems immediately. Sometimes we need to act quickly. Other problems we should give to God or else we can make matters worse. We may say things we can't take back later.

This is not an exact science. We learn as we go. The closer we grow to God, the more we learn discernment and self-control. We become meek, which refers to strength under control. When the storms do hit, the best thing is that we have learned how to return to perfect peace, our joy, trusting that the Lord will turn it around for good. "Trust in the Lord with all your heart and do not lean on your own understanding" (Proverbs 3:5).

When we jump in with both feet we learn to trust and have faith since we don't know what's happening on the other side of the wall, or down the road, or across town. But God does!

1 John 2:27 says, "As for you, the anointing which you received from Him abides in you, and you have no need for anyone to teach you; but as His anointing teaches you about all things, and is true and is not a lie, and just as it has taught you, you abide in Him."

The Holy Spirit will teach us "how and when" to deal with a problem and how to handle situations with God's help. We now lean on Him for direction because He knows best, even if we have to wait for Him to reveal the answer to us. Psalm 27:14 advises, "Wait for the Lord; Be strong and let your heart take courage; Yes, wait for the Lord."

The more we submerge ourselves in the Lord, the stronger

we become. Our spirits are flooded by His holiness. We can remain spiritually submerged and never have to "come up for air" like when we are submerged in water! Spiritual submerging is just the opposite.

We learn to walk with God, slowly at first, by reading the Bible. That's like dipping in our big toe. Eventually, we begin to build a relationship with Him in faith and trust. That's like going in waist deep.

We now have a source to answer all our questions. Some questions only God can answer. His ways are better than our ways. Isaiah 55:8-9 puts it this way: "For My thoughts are not your thoughts, nor are your ways My ways," declares the LORD. For as the heavens are higher than the earth, so are My ways higher than your ways and My thoughts than your thoughts."

When we start feeling God's love in our hearts, our spirits begin moving in sync with His Spirit and we become one together with Him. "But the one who joins himself to the Lord is one spirit with Him" (1 Corinthians 6:17). We're all the way in now! And remember, we don't have to come up for air – we can stay spiritually submerged! We have finally jumped in with both feet. Now being submerged becomes our NEW COMFORT ZONE, our new natural state.

PART 3 - DEVELOPING DISCIPLINE

Of course, since we are still made of flesh and blood, we will sometimes be tempted to react to life's turmoil as we did in the past. But thankfully, things are not the same! Now we will feel led by the Holy Spirit to respond in ways that please God. 1 Timothy 6:11 instructs us: "Flee from these things, you man of God, and pursue righteousness, godliness, faith, love, perseverance and gentleness."

Our old behaviors will seem unnatural to us because we're

not the same people anymore – we are new creations. As 2 Corinthians 5:17 explains, "Therefore if anyone is in Christ, he is a new creature; the old things passed away; behold, new things have come."

I'll tell you, disciplining yourself is frustrating and hard - sometimes CRAZY hard! For me, the major thing I needed to conquer was my addiction to drugs and alcohol. I conquered it (with help, of course), but I've been finding out that it's not the end of my growth as a Christian. I thought I was finished, done; wasn't that enough? But now I have other areas to conquer and I get mad – come on, really?!

I had to quit smoking, start dieting, develop a new sleeping pattern…when does it end?! The answer is, it's never enough because God has more work to do in me! So, now I see what I need to do. I have to accept this with a joyful heart and change my attitude toward discipline because it is NOT THE ENEMY!

Think of yourself as a plant in God's garden. Sometimes it is necessary to prune foliage to eliminate the dead stuff. We should not continue to drag around unnecessary weight in our walk with the Lord! The writer of Hebrews 12:27 explains it this way: "The removing of those things which can be shaken, as of created things, so that those things which cannot be shaken may remain."

When we hear God's words and apply them to our lives, we show wisdom and gain benefits. When we follow God's ways, we are building a strong foundation that is secure and won't ever be destroyed. Jesus said, "Therefore everyone who hears these words of Mine and acts on them, may be compared to a wise man who built his house on the rock" (Matthew 7:24).

"Therefore, my beloved brethren, be steadfast, immovable, always abounding in the work of the Lord, knowing that your toil is not in vain in the Lord" (1 Corinthians 15:58).

Building Your Lifes New Strong foundation

- put GOD first
- Prov.4:5-27 · Knowledge of Gods Word
- Apply GODS Word in your life
- GODS Word will give you Wisdom
- Make a commitment
- Make and form good Habits
- Fellowship with GODS people
- Forgive yourself and others
- Dedicate your life to GODS Ways
- Learn to be Grateful for all things
- Surround your self with good people
- Stay Away from Evil Prov.4:27
- pray to your Lord God, Have faith in Gods Word. Love your Lord with all your HEART Soul

CHAPTER 2

BECOMING BALANCED

PART 1 - THE PROMISE

"O taste and see that the LORD is good; How blessed is the man who takes refuge in Him!" (Psalm 34:8).

The Bible is our lifeline, our air supply, our road map, a blueprint to a healthy, happy, and complete way of life. It stirs up our true being, answers who, what, where, and why, and shows us the right path and direction we should go. It gives us a true character and the right values we should combine to cultivate in our everyday lives.

It replaces what is lost, fills the emptiness that plagues us, replaces bad habits with overwhelming successes, sets us on high, pulls us up from the infernal destruction. It takes away our limitations and replaces them with grand possibilities. The promises are our right to claim. It takes back our rightful place – a daughter or son of the Most High.

The knowledge of God is the key to reclaiming our position in life. We sift out what hinders us from pursuing our rightful place. It frees us. We don't have to be enslaved by unhealthy paths, roads, decisions, bad habits, pain, guilt, and all kinds of sufferings. We have a guide.

We are never alone, abandoned. We find joy and happiness in our hearts and souls. We have hope again.

There are three parts to a human being – body, soul, and spirit. These three parts need to be in sync (balanced) with each other. Otherwise, there will be much conflict and it can actually be dangerous to our overall well-being.

This story reflects my personal journey that should be considered and then applied to one's own life. I am offering you an invitation, a "ticket" so to speak.

John 14:26 tells us, "But the Helper, the Holy Spirit, whom the Father will send in My name, He will teach you all things, and bring to your remembrance all that I said to you."

I had to abandon everything I knew and thought I loved – in fact, couldn't live without – all I ever counted on that gave me comfort. However, it was all false security. I wasn't even the person I thought I was – one who was ridiculed, had many hang-ups and addictions, and believed she was unworthy. The shame and guilt had kept me chained to a life that God never intended for me.

Just like an old building, I had to be torn down. The only way for me to be rebuilt in the right way was to be built up into God's ways. Otherwise, my own ways and thoughts would have kept me chained to that old foundation, stuck in the same circumstances, going in wrong directions, making repetitive mistakes.

The way I was raised, lived, saw things, learned things, experienced things, was the way of the world. I was conditioned to believe this was normal and I didn't even know there was another way besides mine. For example, I knew nothing about honesty. God's ways were definitely not my ways.

I was introduced to God at the worst time of my life. However, that is where I needed to be. Otherwise, I wouldn't have been ready to clean my slate and be prepared in mind and spirit to be rebuilt into God's way. It felt right learning God's truth by reading His words in the Bible. I was open and ready to have God show me who I really was. So, I invited the Holy Spirit into my heart. At that point, the Holy Spirit took over.

2 Peter 1:4 says, "He has granted to us His precious and magnificent promises, so that by them you may become partakers of the divine nature, having escaped the corruption that is in the world by lust."

Since we were all created by God, we were all designed to be capable of having a relationship with Him. We become His children through accepting Jesus as Lord.

Like many people, I would sometimes think about getting an inheritance from my parents when they passed away. But being close to God, living with His intentions and purpose, is like already having your inheritance in this life! With the Lord, not only do we already have it – we NEVER LOSE IT. Just like with Aaron in Numbers 18:20, the Lord says, "I am your portion and your inheritance…." We are also like Levi in Deuteronomy 10:9: "The LORD is his inheritance."

PART 2 - JIGSAW PUZZLE

God gives me illustrations to demonstrate that life is better when we look at things through His eyes and follow His instructions. Like a jigsaw puzzle, God has already laid out all the pieces we need to live an unshaken, steady, well-adjusted, balanced life. Reading the Bible and listening to the Holy Spirit will guide us on fitting the pieces together and building our lives.

How we apply His instructions will determine whether we will live the abundant lives he intended for us. This does not mean we won't have any troubles – WE WILL – but we're now better prepared.

Ephesians 6:10-11 encourages us: "Finally, be strong in the Lord and in the strength of His might. Put on the full armor of God, so that you will be able to stand firm against the schemes of the devil."

The idea is to use only God's pieces to complete the jigsaw puzzle of our lives. If we are successful in this, the world's "pieces" (troubles, mayhem, destruction, pain, worry, etc.) won't fit into our life's puzzle! They won't "stick" and will eventually fall away.

PART 3 - THE HOLY SPIRIT SPEAKS

A connection is now initiated between God's Holy Spirit and our spirit, like an infusion. The Spirit begins to direct us. When we get off the right path, the Spirit, like a gentle hand, moves us back where we belong.

The mind is key. We acquire the right state of mind when we read the Word of God. It seeps into us through our spiritual pores. It becomes alive in us as the indwelling Holy Spirit is awakened. Then we start to hear God's voice speaking into our spirit! It's different from the usual voice, which is just our own subconscious speaking. Over time we learn to hear God speak.

Now, for the first time, we are able to act on God's voice as if it were our own. In the past, when we heard only our own inner voice, the thought would just pass away. But now, when God is speaking into our spirit, we can tell the difference. If we don't act on what He has said, the voice will linger on and "nag" us. We won't be able to put Him off as we did with our own thoughts, placing them on a back burner.

After we accomplish the task that God has told us to do, then we feel the life, joy, and peace that God gives us to show His approval of our discipline in acting out that obedience.

This is how God moves through us and talks to us. We need to be open. We should want to shine His light forth to others by becoming His vessel. Psalm 119:105 proclaims, "Your word is a lamp to my feet and a light to my path."

When I was first in the process of learning about the Lord, things were changing suddenly and noticeably to me and to others.

Each believer receives at least one extraordinary spiritual gift from God. Romans 12:6 explains, "Since we have gifts that differ according to the grace given to us, each of us is to exercise them accordingly."

Let me elaborate – this is an honor, a life-changing event! Listen to this verse from Romans 12:1-2: "Therefore I urge you, brethren, by the mercies of God, to present your bodies a living and holy sacrifice, acceptable to God, which is your spiritual service of worship. And do not be conformed to this world, but be transformed by the renewing of your mind, so that you may prove what the will of God is, that which is good and acceptable and perfect."

Over time, our gifts become more fully developed. Also, we become better able to differentiate between our own thoughts versus the thoughts that originate from His Spirit. It's not an exact science. Everyone's timetable is different. As mentioned in Romans 12:6 above, God gives us gifts to exercise in proportion to His grace and our faith, so we don't get overwhelmed.

This part of my relationship with God is a "trip" for me! All of a sudden, without any notice, God speaks to my spirit and I feel overcome by Him. I gain the strength and whatever confidence I need to follow through with the Word He has given me.

For example: I was on the bus, and a man was sitting on the other side of me. Well, God spoke to my spirit and told me to tell this man, 'You're a good man, and you have a word for someone that will help their situation. Please don't hold back on telling it to that person."

So now what do you do!? Tell yourself, "Okay, I'm just losing it"? No, you can't brush this off, because every fiber of your being is confirming this is God's will. And by now you know the difference! You are aware of His Spirit speaking to your mind. Faith, hope, and love are needed, and love is what holds it all together. Love can change everything. 1 Corinthians 13:13 says, "But now faith, hope, love, abide these three; but the greatest of these is love."

So at this point, I stand up on the bus. My obedience to God is more important to me than what this stranger will think of me. That's one way you know for sure that God is "infused" in your life. For me, this is the most important part of my life – putting God's will first. My prayer is that it becomes yours as well.

Listen to the words Jesus spoke in Matthew 22:37-38: "You shall love the Lord your God with all your heart, and with all your soul, and with all your mind. This is the great and foremost commandment."

It's similar to sowing seed. The more we obey His will and do as He asks, the more our relationship with Him deepens. Our love for Him grows. We want to dig deeper spiritually, because we know there's so much more.

We keep seeking God because we learn that His ways are like a deep river of rushing water that continually cleanses us from ourselves – washing us clean from our self-centeredness, our egos, our impurities, everything that stops us from becoming what we should have been…opening our hearts to love we never had or imagined. We gain a warmth of security, knowing who we really are and where we stand – on holy ground. We should never want to resurrect our old selves, longing instead to forever remain as children of God.

PART 4 - LAST WORDS

We take to heart people's last wills and testaments, final words, last wishes, and deathbed confessions before they draw their dying breath. Death row inmates are offered a last meal of their choice. Well, if we take these last words of a person's life seriously, then what about taking our Lord and Savior's last words to heart?

Jesus knew beforehand that He was going to be crucified. As a result, all His words and teachings were, in essence, His last words to the people to whom He spoke. They would become a part of the inspired scriptures of the Bible. He was setting the stage, so to speak.

Jesus told his parents who He really was at the age of twelve, after the Feast of Passover. He told them that He was the Son of God. "And He said to them, 'Why is it that you were looking for Me? Did you not know that I had to be in My Father's house?'" (Luke 2:49).

Likewise, the Gospel of John 13:3 also sets the stage: "Jesus, knowing that the Father had given all things into His hands, and that He had come forth from God and was going back to God."

Everything spoken by Jesus in Scripture can be accepted as His written last words to us. He knew His mission was to become a sacrifice for us and pay the penalty for our sins.

According to Proverbs 18:21, "Death and life are in the power of the tongue, and those who love it will eat its fruit." We can rest assured that every word that proceeded out of the mouth of Jesus is true. If we believe in our hearts that God's words are for our benefit, why then do we not listen, read, study, and live by them?

"All Scripture is inspired by God and profitable for teaching, for reproof, for correction, for training in righteousness; so that the man of God may be adequate, equipped for every good work" (2 Timothy 3:16-17).

Listen to the words of Jesus in Luke 11:28: "But He said, 'On the contrary, blessed are those who hear the word of God and observe it.'" When we honor God, we in turn also edify ourselves, our lives, values, family, and children.

There is so much wrong with this world, so much heartbreak, so many things that are out of our control, that it's easy for us to get lost in its corruption. But if we love and trust God, we believe He is always in control, even when things seem to be falling apart. God has us! We just have to take a back seat and have faith.

God gives us the strength to endure our struggles so we should take heart:

"'For I know the plans that I have for you,' declares the Lord, 'plans for welfare and not for calamity, to give you a future and a hope'" (Jeremiah 29:11).

If we would consider what Jesus wants us to do in the same way we try to carry out a dying person's wishes, we will do well. We should learn what the King of Kings wants us to know. Proverbs 16:20 says, "He who gives attention to the word will find good, and blessed is he who trusts in the LORD."

His words are life and a life-giving fountain to those who possess it.

PART 5 - DEATH AND LIFE ARE IN THE POWER OF THE TONGUE

A kind word, a million dollars, and everything in between

When someone is on a bridge ready to jump and end his or her life, what's best at that moment in time – the million dollars or a kind word, a word of hope, a word of encouragement to deter the person from ending his or her life?

When we sow seeds, we don't know which ones will grow. Our spoken words have power so it's important to always speak wisely, encouragingly, and supportively. The Bible tells us that "death and life are in the power of the tongue" (Proverbs 18:21).

Even for ourselves, thinking healthy, positive thoughts can change everything and brighten up the day. What we surround ourselves with will help us create what we want and will influence how we express ourselves to others. God doesn't want our thoughts clouded up – He wants us to think clearly. "For God has not given us a spirit of timidity, but of power and love and discipline" (2 Timothy 1:7).

When we think positively, we will make better choices. We will feel good about ourselves and will want good for others. Romans 12:2 says, "And do not be conformed to this world, but be transformed by the renewing of your mind, so that you may prove what the will of God is, that which is good and acceptable and perfect."

This takes practice. I still catch myself not thinking correctly on occasion. But when the will of God becomes our priority, God's Spirit reminds us. It's kind of like riding a bicycle. Our souls and spirits start becoming in sync with God. It's a glorious feeling that results in rewards all the days of our lives.

"Cling to what is good" (Romans 12:9).

"Be devoted to one another in brotherly love; give preference to one another in honor" (Romans 12:10).

Our actions and words have a ripple effect, knowingly or unknowingly. Therefore, everything that comes out of our mouths should be spoken out of love.

"Therefore, laying aside falsehood, speak truth each one of you with his neighbor, for we are members of one another" (Ephesians 4:25).

We have the power given to us by God to help change a person's path, to guide them to life, a life worth saving. We do this because we love God and that's what He wants from us. Try your best to make disciples from an honest heart.

Now listen! Our God is awesome. He blesses us for carrying out His will.

Exodus 19:5 encourages us, "Now then, if you will indeed obey My voice and keep My covenant, then you shall be My own possession among all the peoples, for all the earth is Mine."

PART 6 - DO NOT BE UNEQUALLY YOKED

Saving your family through your obedience to the Lord

"God remembered Noah" (Genesis 8:1). Noah found favor with the Lord with the result that all his family members were saved from the flood that destroyed every other living thing on earth. This happened because Noah was a righteous man, blameless in his time. In fact, Noah is described as having "walked with God" (Genesis 6:9).

If you're having trouble drawing near to God, don't give up. He lives within every believer. It is we who fail to seek Him wholeheartedly. He gives us choices. If we choose Him, we can activate His Holy Spirit that lives within us. God promises that if we obey Him blessings will follow. Listen to what is written in Joshua 1:8: "This book of the law shall not depart from your mouth, but you shall meditate on it day and night, so that you may be careful to do according to all that is written in it; for then you will make your way prosperous, and then you will have success."

Jesus said in John 14:21, "He who has My commandments and keeps them is the one who loves Me; and he who loves Me will be loved by My Father, and I will love him and will disclose Myself to him."

And this is the truth. I am personally a witness to these statements. God has revealed Himself to me. Others around me have witnessed God showering His gifts, His blessings, and His favor upon my life. I, in turn, write this because it is what I want most for you, your family, and loved ones.

As we mature in the Lord, we may need to let some people in our lives go. Here is what is written in 2 Corinthians 6:14: "Do not be bound together with unbelievers; for what partnership have righteousness and lawlessness, or what fellowship has light with darkness?"

We know that our relationship with the Lord is strengthening when we are consistently losing interest in people who aren't following God's ways. They will become more distant, and we're okay with that now. We come to realize that those people and that old way of life are fading and becoming less and less important. Our preferences are now different because what

God wants excites us more than what our old friends think or feel about us. That former lifestyle is no longer attractive or interesting to us anymore. We care about them and should try to help them find God's way; but if they remain reluctant, it's okay to let them go.

Being equally yoked is a part of being well-built - able to exhibit self-control when responding to stimuli, being pulled together, fitted, matched, or joined, able to perceive the same stimuli and/or conditions.

Matthew 11:29-30 says, "Take My yoke upon you and learn from Me, for I am gentle and humble in heart, and you will find rest for your souls. For My yoke is easy and My burden is light." This is a part of following the Lord.

As God's will begins to fill our minds and hearts with its importance, our souls begin to feel contented and our new outlook on life (through God's eyes) brings a new path of peace. This new path becomes the way we see things, talk, think, and walk through life.

"Make my joy complete by being of the same mind, maintaining the same love, united in spirit, intent on one purpose" (Philippians 2:2).

What's really incredible is the more we learn of God and walk in His ways, the more we start cultivating the art of hearing His voice. We learn the difference between our own thoughts and His spirit speaking to us. We no longer act on our own impulses, but now we're directed by the Holy Spirit's touch, voice, knowledge, and "nudge." It is no longer our own will that directs us but the will of God.

Isn't this just incredibly powerful?! The Almighty has entered our innermost being simply because we invited Him to do so! Now we will never be the same – never alone – and His joy and peace will attract others into our path.

"For you once were not a people, but now you are the people of God; you had not received mercy, but now you have received mercy" (1 Peter 2:10).

Once His Spirit sweeps over your soul, you can feel the Holy Spirit as He takes control. Your head may even spin from feeling a little light-headed. You feel the stirrings in your soul. Your God is loving you and touching you to the deepest depths of your soul, and uncontrollable tears of joy may spring forth from your eyes. Your heart might pump a little faster and you may even have to catch your breath a time or two. You feel radiant knowing it's God's Holy Spirit filling every part of your soul with an unspeakable joy. You might feel a trembling or shaking, but one characterized by complete contentment. You are becoming one with the Lord.

Know without a doubt, deep in your heart of hearts, that God has touched you in a way only He can.

If you earnestly seek God, you will find all that you've ever longed for. He will fulfill the deepest yearnings of your heart. If you follow His ways, He will bring completion to your life and destiny. He will turn you into the person you were always meant to be by His design. You will become strong, knowing the truth and becoming a light for others. Your light will shine light on others' paths. You will lead others to the source of eternal life – salvation through Jesus Christ. And you will be rewarded, blessed, and favored of the Lord!

CHAPTER 3

GAINING WISDOM

"But the wisdom from above is first pure, then peaceable, gentle, reasonable, full of mercy and good fruits, unwavering, without hypocrisy. And the seed whose fruit is righteousness is sown in peace by those who make peace" (James 3:17-18).

When you start forming a relationship with God, after a while you will fall in love with the kindness of His character. We learn how much He loves us and what He had His Son do for us.

We finally have a relationship in this life that can NEVER disappoint us, fail us, wrong us, abandon us, or lie to us. No one can ever rob us of this awesome love. We're always surrounded by it. It leads us to places we never thought we'd experience.

Gradually, we surround ourselves with others who have developed this same relationship. Our lives are pruned and given a shape conforming to our new level of growth. We are now able to deal with what we once thought were major issues – they become bumps in the road and are easily removed or negotiated. God's acceptance gives us peace, even when we're in uncomfortable circumstances. His peace is also accompanied by His wisdom.

Proverbs 3:7 cautions us, "Do not be wise in your own eyes; fear the Lord and turn away from evil." Wisdom means sometimes accepting ways with which we don't agree. We don't need to see eye to eye with the Lord every time. If we stop trying to be in control and figure things out, but instead let God take control, life can then be guided by His direction. When this happens, our hearts will be less troubled and fearful.

Jesus comforted His disciples in the Gospel of John 14:27: "Peace I leave with you; My peace I give to you; not as the world gives do I give to you. Do not let your heart be troubled, nor let it be fearful."

PART 1 - THE PROBLEMS

The problems in our lives keep on coming like the mail carrier or a train running on its schedule. Neither snow, nor rain, nor heat, nor gloom of night stays our problems from the swift completion of their appointed rounds! No, we're never going to escape the trials and problems of our lives!

That's one reason we should plant the roots of our lives deep in God. When these problems come, we know that we have access to the correct resources to handle any storm. Instead of dwelling on our problems, we can now act on what God's Word says.

"And the peace of God, which surpasses all comprehension, will guard your hearts and your minds in Christ Jesus. Finally, brethren, whatever is true, whatever is honorable, whatever is right, whatever is pure, whatever is lovely, whatever is of good repute, if there is any excellence and if anything worthy of praise, dwell on these things" (Philippians 4:7-8).

In a rehab facility, residents are given sobriety tools to ward off the urges of addiction, like a flea collar on a cat. Well, God's Word is like that for me! When we wear God's Word around our necks, surrounding our lives, the demons have to flee! At least, it's the way I see things.

Proverbs 3:3 says, "Do not let kindness and truth leave you; bind them around your neck, write them on the tablet of your heart."

I used to allow the problems in my life to paralyze me; and as most people do, I would look to my friends and loved ones for help and advice. But like an infection - if help and advice aren't coming from the correct source (God's love and guidance), the problem will simply spread and worsen like cancer. Whereas following God's direction will bring wisdom into our hearts and peace into our souls.

"Discretion will guard you, understanding will watch over you, to deliver you from the way of evil" (Proverbs 2:11-12).

When you take a car into the repair shop, forget it! You're at its mercy. The shop can tell you anything and if you don't have the relevant knowledge and education, you'll pay! In other words, we can't rely on the people living in the world (not walking with the Lord) to help us with our problems or we'll pay!!! Proverbs 3:13 tells us, "How blessed is the man who finds wisdom and the man who gains understanding." I always got into deeper trouble by taking my own advice, without seeking the counsel of God.

Since I gave my life over to the will of God, I am reminded of the classic movie *The Wizard of Oz*. After Dorothy's house landed in Oz following the tornado, she opened the door and looked out. Suddenly, Dorothy and all the members of the audience were amazed by the spectacular colors! Remember, that movie was released on August 25, 1939, when there was no color television. Viewers of that time were captivated, enamored, and blown away by the beauty, delight, allure, riveting wonder, charm, and attractiveness seen by Dorothy when she opened that door. This example is the best way for me to describe the feeling of giving myself over to the will and care of Father God.

For me, I'm just in total awe, and it never goes away. Once you experience this "eclipse" (blotting out of your old life), you'll never be the same. There's no going back – the dark part of your life doesn't excite you anymore. Just as during an eclipse when the light of the sun or moon starts to reappear, the new you is born. This feeling of God's love, grace, and mercy never fades – it only becomes stronger.

"Therefore if anyone is in Christ, he is a new creature; the old things passed away; behold, new things have come" (2 Corinthians 5:17).

Problems will come and keep on coming, but with our amazing God and the trust we have in Him, our fears will subside. Like a person in a batting cage, the balls are being thrown at us – but we have a Batter who hits the balls out of the park! God is our Batter and our Protector. 2 Thessalonians 3:3 states, "The Lord is faithful, and He will strengthen and protect you from the evil one." To put it another way, we see a wall of problems, but God sees the bigger picture that includes the solutions.

I'm just an ordinary person, but I have to tell you that my many years of being an addict taught me one extremely important lesson. My ways of approaching life and its problems are insufficient because I don't have the divine wisdom that God has. Unlike us, God has pure motives. He knows the best solution to any and every problem that we will ever face.

Since I've given my life over to God, I have to say that now when I face a problem, I have learned to STOP. Instead of reacting, I ask God for wisdom. James 1:5 advises, "But if any of you lacks wisdom, let him ask of God, who gives to all generously and without reproach, and it will be given to him."

God wants all of us, including you, to find His peace in your life. I am sharing with you what I've learned, but your experiences won't be exactly the same. Not everyone experienced the destruction that I did living such a worldly life, but God is still the answer for you.

"In all your ways acknowledge Him, and He will make your paths straight. Do not be wise in your own eyes; fear the LORD and turn away from evil. It will be healing to your body and refreshment to your bones" (Proverbs 3:6-8).

I have found these verses to be true! Only at this time of my life have I experienced the love God speaks of in His Word. Truly, everything does come together for our good. Blessings truly come upon our lives and our trust in our Lord only deepens. It has happened for me and I want this for you as well.

"Delight yourself in the LORD; and He will give you the desires of your heart" (Psalm 37:4).

PART 2 – LEARNING WHO WE ARE IN CHRIST

As with our automobile, we hold the keys to give the engine life. We have the power to drive the car in the direction of our choice. The fuel we use helps determine the vehicle's performance.

Likewise, we also hold the keys to our own lives, our hearts, and our minds. We have the power to lead our lives in the direction of our choice. The knowledge we apply to fill our minds, hearts, and souls will help to determine our performance.

One of the things that increases a car's value is preventive maintenance. In a similar fashion, our lives require "maintenance." Every car, appliance, and so on is accompanied by a manufacturer's maintenance book that includes instructions and problem-solving suggestions. The purpose is to help you maintain and care for your possessions so they have longer lives.

Well, our lives are even more valuable than our material possessions. We come with an instruction manual and its author is God Himself – God Almighty. And His Son Jesus Christ left us the best example!

"For you have been called for this purpose, since Christ also suffered for you, leaving you an example for you to follow in His steps" (1 Peter 2:21).

Of course, not everyone follows the manual. Some people skip pages and others use a knock-off brand instruction manual or jimmy-rig it out of laziness, not wanting to deal with it. It is up to us to desire to maintain a long, good, high-performance life, giving worth and value to ourselves and our families. Set that good example!

"My son, give attention to my wisdom, incline your ear to my understanding; That you may observe discretion and your lips may reserve knowledge" (Proverbs 5-1:2).

PART 3 – LET GOD DIRECT YOUR STEPS

When we wake up in the morning, it's a fresh new step. We have a great God who knows what our needs are and what's best for us. So, let's check in with Him before we start our day. Let God direct our steps.

When we obtain God's approval and follow His directions we can't fail.
However, our ways are not always in line with His ways. So, if things sometimes don't go as we had hoped and planned, we can still trust God that He has something even better in mind for us. Psalm 32:8 assures us, "I will instruct you and teach you in the way which you should go; I will counsel you with My eye upon you."

As a former addict, I walked in self-destruction (MY ways) for over forty years. Now that I have invited God into my life, heart, and every part of my being, His favor and blessings are upon me.

When I stopped walking in my own ways and began allowing God to direct my ways, a whole new light was turned on and began shining. I'm no longer in the dark stumbling around and falling. My way is clear now. My heart is filled with the love and joy only God can provide. He, God, makes it possible to love and even help the unlovable.

My ex-boyfriend, who was also an addict, left our ten-year relationship for his high school sweetheart. Well, you know, that was a hard one to swallow! After my recovery and after I had developed a strong relationship with my God, forgiveness for him came upon me.

I learned that his new relationship didn't work out because of his addiction, of which she wasn't initially aware. He had found God and needed help. I was able to help him grow in his relationship with the Lord and came alongside him in fighting his addiction until he chose to go into residential treatment. We remain the best of friends. Only with the love of my God could I do this. You see, God's love covers a multitude of sins (1 Peter 4:8). Because of this, I saw my ex-boyfriend through God's eyes and no longer through my eyes.

Once you allow God to direct your steps, unbelievable blessings follow. Others will start to see His favor upon your life. And in turn, you can become this marvelous person you were originally intended to be. With God blessing your life, you yourself can serve others as a disciple of Christ. You can help lead them to God by directing them to His life, His path, and His guidance.

"In all your ways acknowledge Him, and He will make your paths straight. Do not be wise in your own eyes" (Proverbs 3:6-7).

God intended for Him to be our lifeline. The umbilical

cord is the life support system for the developing body of a baby, providing the necessary food supply and oxygen. Well, we can apply this way of thinking to our spiritual lives. God's words supply the "nutrients and oxygen" needed to develop our minds, feed our spirits, access His qualities, and receive His "DNA."

"God created man in His own image, in the image of God He created him; male and female He created them" (Genesis 1:27).

To find true joy, we have to tear down our old fleshly selves and start rebuilding ourselves into God's image, the way He intended for us to be. God created the world from just a word, and His Word will not return void. As it is written in Isaiah 55:11, "So will My word be which goes forth from My mouth; it will not return to Me empty, without accomplishing what I desire, and without succeeding in the matter for which I sent it."

We inherit the power to exercise the will of God when we connect our lives to His life via the spiritual "umbilical cord" of God's Word, His support system. It's as if His power is injected into us. God gives us a choice to receive and act on this power. Those who choose not to are canceling out the gifts God intended them to have. They will feel lost and will suffer the cruelties of life alone.

God is always waiting for us to come to Him. He's always waiting on us; He never changes. When we finally decide to look at ourselves as God's children created by Him and for Him (in His image), we will behave and think differently.

Once we choose to live for God and stop living for ourselves, we have a responsibility to learn God's ways for our lives. We should eagerly desire to learn His ways, absorbing them like a sponge absorbs liquids! The more we act on what we learn, we should see that we're becoming more Christlike. We're growing in the characteristics that He placed inside us through the "download" of the Holy Spirit.

Think of a bodybuilder. We are all born with muscles, but if we faithfully exercise our bodies day by day, eventually we will witness the growth and definition of those muscles. Likewise, we are no longer foreigners but have become members of God's family. He placed in us everything He has to give us when we received His Holy Spirit. We just need to develop it.

We also know that when an athlete stops exercising, the muscles atrophy. It is just as important for children of God to continue to develop their relationship with Him.

At some point in our lives we "get it." We know that we know that without God, we will never be complete and will always feel a lack, a desire never fulfilled. We realize that only God can fill ALL our voids. It's not even open to question anymore. We absolutely KNOW that we need God Almighty. Only our Heavenly Father can supply all our needs.

CHAPTER 4

A GOOD STATE OF MIND

PART 1 – BE THANKFUL IN EVERYTHING

Thankfulness is the glue that keeps us close and strong in our Lord. God gives us all we need for the particular time in which we live.

I made my own personal list of things for which I am thankful. For example:

1) A grateful heart	6) God directs my steps
2) God forgave me	7) God placed angels over me
3) I have eternal life	8) God's protection
4) God chose me	9) I have good people in my life
5) God supplies my needs	10) God loves me

We can experience God's favor at any time, any moment, all the time. God will give us what we need for our lives at the time we need it. Psalm 34:10 assures us, "But they who seek the Lord shall not be in want of any good thing."

When we are grateful, the peace of Christ is upon us. Anything that tries to hinder our peace gets removed, because the love of our Father God becomes our center. So, could something as simple as gratitude affect our physical and emotional health? Yes! Actually, thankfulness has been proven to be beneficial to our health! A grateful attitude will give us a healthier heart, improved moods, better sleep, and a boosted immune system.

Before I found God, I just rolled with everything, thinking, "This is just the way life is." As a result, I never matured emotionally. I didn't treat people as well as I should have, not knowing myself what true love was. As I came to know our dear Lord, I realized the love He has for us: "Know the love of Christ which surpasses knowledge, that you may be filled up to all the fullness of God" (Ephesians 3:19).

God will never leave us. Once we realize we're called to His purpose, He will work out all the details of our lives. We need not fear. We cast our anxieties on Him, knowing His Spirit dwells in our hearts. This response frees us to be thankful all the time, even when storms come. We are "rooted and grounded in love" (Ephesians 3:17). Hebrews 13:5 describes this as "being content with what you have; for He Himself has said, 'I will never desert you, nor will I ever forsake you.'"

God's Holy Spirit is sustaining us, and we can depend on always having access to Him. Since we're now standing firm in the place we belong, we can reach out to others to help them realize their proper position in life. One of the best feelings we could ever experience is finding total contentment within ourselves, knowing our hearts and minds are right with God – and having the confidence that we're doing our absolute best for ourselves and others.

We are true to ourselves now and free of the devil's lies. This is a major change from our old lives where unexpected, sudden challenges would have sent us back to the world's solutions, like drugs or alcohol, to cover our hurt feelings.

When we are grounded in God's truth, the Helper (the Holy Spirit) reminds us how to deal with life's messes. We will act in a manner that brings out the best in us and others and gives the glory to God! We will also have the wisdom to know when to back out of dead-end situations that try to destroy our well-being.

PART 2 - IT'S NOT A FAIRY TALE

Remember the fairytale books we were read as children? - perhaps even the same ones we now read to our children and grandchildren. At the end of the story it usually reads, "…and they lived happily ever after."

Well, the Bible is truly our "happily ever after." We are forgiven from sin. We're not in darkness anymore. We're able to reveal truth to others. We're dead to sin. Our hearts can feel peace and joy now.

It's one thing to know of God, and another to actually KNOW God. I always knew of God and His Son Jesus. I continued to learn about God through the years. I used to think, "Yes, that's nice we have a God who made us, but He's far away and doesn't really participate in our daily lives." I went as far as to believe that there's a God and his Son who died for us. I figured, "Just do good and when you die, you have a chance to go to heaven."

Then life happens with its pain, destruction, helplessness, and all that. It seems as if God disappears bit by bit into the cloud of hopelessness. We become lost in all of it, and we tend to lose sight of what God and life are really all about. In short, it's a very dark and evil world without having the true knowledge of God.

When I got lost in the tragedies of life, it was as if my awareness of God got lost as well.

Now, it's exactly the opposite. I draw closer to God each and every time opposition finds me. God has become my anchor! I no longer sink into depression nor do I withdraw or relapse into addiction. Instead, I celebrate my trust in God and hold on tight to my faith in Him. And I have learned that having wise Christian friends will build me up.

"He who walks with wise men will be wise, but the companion of fools will suffer harm" (Proverbs 13:20).

God's Word offers us a real chance at a wonderful, beautiful, abundant life. We're able to remove the film of the world off our eyes so we can see clearly. This clarity enables us to leave the world's filth, lies, sin, anger, depressions, and anxiety behind.

The fairy tale becomes our new reality, and our "happily ever after" is now everlasting life with our Lord Jesus. We learn His ways and make them our ways. We take a stand against the devil's tricks and scams, standing on God's truths and promises.

God's book, the Bible, is part of our "happily ever after." Read and study it! Did you know that YOU are in it? God has mentioned you personally! He knew you before you were born! He loves you and wants the best for you.

"Thus says the Lord, your Redeemer, and the one who formed you from the womb, 'I, the Lord, am the maker of all things, stretching out the heavens by Myself and spreading out the earth all alone'" (Isaiah 44:24).

The Lord God gives His knowledge to the ones truly looking for Him. 1 Corinthians 2:12 says, "Now we have received, not the spirit of the world, but the Spirit who is from God, so that we may know the things freely given to us by God."

In the long run, there's nothing to fear when we're in the Lord – even death. Jesus assures us in Luke 9:24, "For whoever wishes to save his life will lose it, but whoever loses his life for My sake, he is the one who will save it." For those who die "in Christ," death means a union with the Lord. When Jesus hung on the cross He cried out, "'Father, into your hands I commit My spirit.' Having said this, He breathed His last" (Luke 23:46).

Therefore, we always have confidence in God in this life, in our troubles, in our death, in our everything. Jesus Himself said, "I am the Light of the world; he who follows Me will not walk in the darkness, but will have the Light of life" (John 8:12).

Truly, we are surrounded by an enormous amount of love right under our noses! Remember though, our Lord is Spirit. We should not look at life through our eyes, but rather through His Spirit that He placed in us. We look to Him by that same Spirit. Romans 8:9 tells us, "You are not in the flesh but in the Spirit, if indeed the Spirit of God dwells in you. But if anyone does not have the Spirit of Christ, he does not belong to Him."

God's Spirit did not come alive in me until I chose to seek Him. It had lain dormant because I allowed the troubles of this world to bury God's Spirit. Eventually, I started yearning for His Spirit to come alive within my spirit and came to the point where I was ready for His Spirit to be ignited in my life!

"In the same way the Spirit also helps our weakness; for we do not know how to pray as we should, but the Spirit Himself intercedes for us with groanings too deep for words; and He who searches the hearts knows what the mind of the Spirit is, because He intercedes for the saints according to the will of God" (Romans 8:26-27).

It's an amazing thing to be adopted by God! We become children of God! For me, it was everything I needed, everything I was looking for – the simplicity of a life that's pure, fresh, sparkling, and so wholesome and clean.

And truthfully, isn't this what we're all looking for? This world is a mess and will continue to be so. But we who seek the Lord can be made complete by His love.

Jesus said, "Ask, and it will be given to you; seek, and you will find; knock, and it will be opened to you. For everyone who asks receives, and he who seeks finds, and to him who knocks it will be opened" (Matthew 7:7-8).

God IS our happily ever after…and our "happily ever after" can begin right now!

PART 3 – REPLACE IT

When we start replacing our burdens with reliance on God's direction in our lives, we're building and strengthening the image of God we reflect to others. As mentioned in Chapter 2, Part 2, "Jigsaw Puzzle," we have now replaced our negativity, depression, and doubts with the knowledge of who we really are in Christ Jesus. We begin experiencing the peace and joy that were robbed from us.

We become what we believe. How we think, our belief system, impacts our lives and actions. As we learn to become more consistent in our Christian walk, we grow strong spiritually. We set our minds on wanting "the things from above," which are now more important than the world's demands. As stated in Colossians 3:2, "Set your mind on the things above, not on the things that are on earth."

Our new behavior develops into a pattern. We are now able to display a very powerful, positive influence on others. Even placing others' needs above our own is very helpful in our walk with the Lord. Remember, according to Jesus, the second greatest commandment is to love your neighbor as yourself (Matthew 22:39). Witnessing the joy we add to someone else's life is like witnessing a miracle!

We can become one with God's Spirit. We learn to think God's thoughts. We're willing to strip away our old selves! We do this by constantly "replacing" our old ways/thoughts with the Lord's. When we get weary, the Spirit, the Holy Ghost, helps us by nudging us in the right direction.

Colossians 3:15 sets an attainable goal for the believer: "Let the peace of Christ rule in your hearts, to which indeed you were called in one body; and be thankful."

More and more we look at life through God's eyes. More and more we're filled with His contentment and His love. We know in our heart of hearts that we're okay, and we're always going to be okay no matter what! In whatever problems we face, God's face will always shine upon us. (Check out the beautiful high priestly blessing found in Numbers 6:24-26.)

"The righteous cry, and the Lord hears and delivers them out of all their troubles" (Psalm 34:17).

If we are consistently walking in healthy spiritual paths, we will be able to do everything Jesus Christ calls us to do. Philippians 4:13 encourages me that "I can do all things through Him who strengthens me."

Our old lives with the associated lifestyles have been superseded. God's thoughts have replaced our former ways of thinking. We can now manage our lives with grace, wellbeing, purity, love, and gentleness, for His Spirit is now leading us and directing us.

"My son, do not forget my teaching, but let your heart keep my commandments; for length of days and years of life and peace they will add to you" (Proverbs 3:1-2).

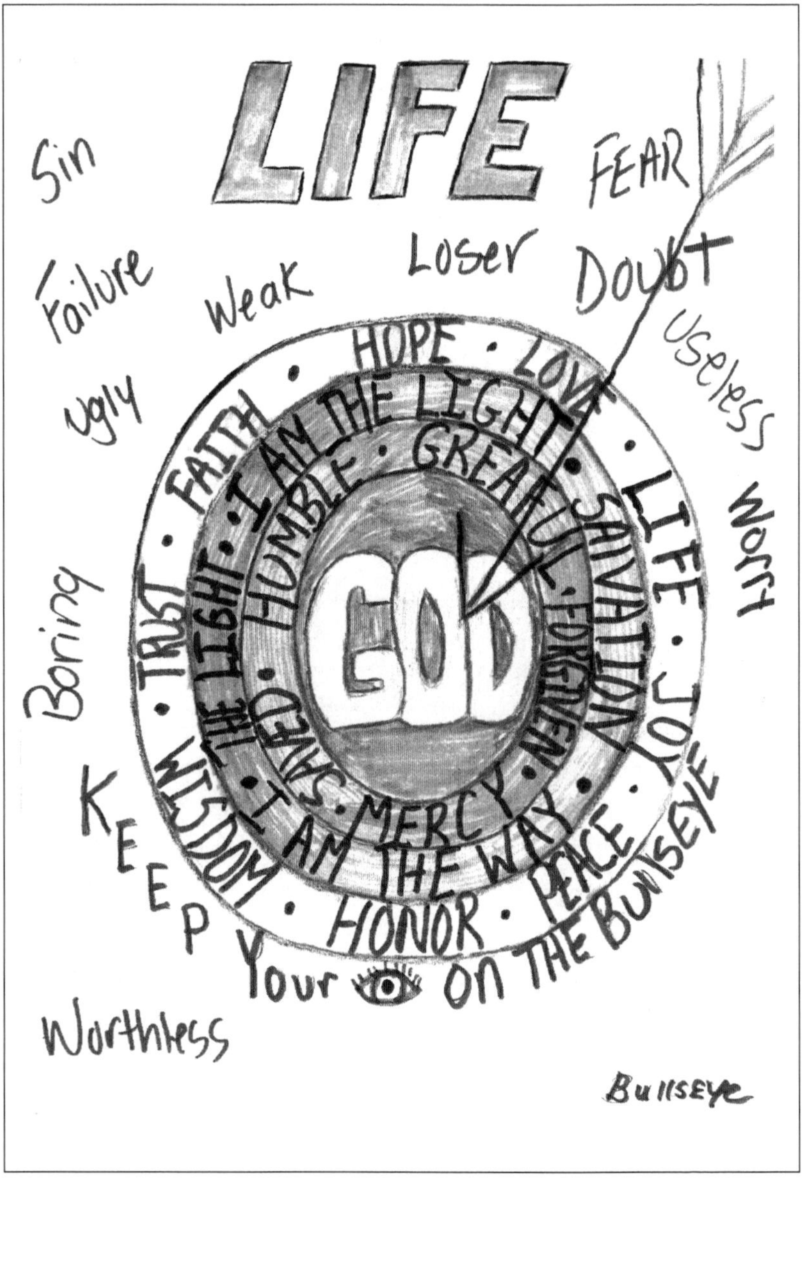
LIFE
Sin
FEAR
Failure
Loser
Doubt
Weak
Useless
ugly
HOPE
LOVE
FAITH
I AM THE LIGHT
HUMBLE
GREATFUL
LIFE
SALVATION
Worry
GOD
Boring
TRUST
THE LIGHT
SAVED
FORGIVEN
JOY
MERCY
WISDOM
I AM THE WAY
HONOR
PEACE
KEEP Your ON THE BULLSEYE
Worthless
Bullseye

CHAPTER 5

RIGHT PRIORITIES

How does an addict develop the right kind of priorities in life? For over forty years, my ONLY priority was my addiction! Trust me, after forty-plus years as an addict you're far and deep into a one-sided outlook on life. That's all you know! That's all you're comfortable with. What and why would you want to change now?

My friends were like my "black sheep family." We accepted each other when no one else would.

My upbringing was Catholic. My mom was "saved." Boy, she loved that Bible and always had my hand on it to solemnly swear I did not steal that money or did not do this or that. Well, I didn't get struck by lightning, so okay, I'm still here. Nothing happened, right?

But something DID happen. Even to this day I still remember where I was, how old I was, and what lies I spoke at the ages of twelve, thirteen, and so on.

Since we're created in God's image, I believe we know when we grieve His Holy Spirit. We can somehow feel the sorrow, distress, and emotional pain we cause God, even without knowing Him on a personal level. Addiction numbs our sensitivity to God, but that sensitivity is also part of our very being that can't be ignored forever.

Even in my addiction, I would look for God by joining churches of different denominations and participating in various Bible studies. My spirit longed for my God. Even in a drunken state I sometimes found myself driving to a church, going in and just sitting in the pew for a while – not knowing why I drove there. I just knew I needed to be there – HAD to be there.

One time a friend asked me about it the next day. She was told I had been in a church, reeking of alcohol. She was upset about it. Of course, she knew I was an alcoholic, but I guess she was confused as to why I showed up to church drunk. Well, back then I didn't know either!

Now as I look back, I have the answer. I know why I drove myself there, even though I was consumed by alcohol. It was because the Holy Spirit took the initiative and influenced me to go there. I see many times in my life when the Holy Spirit reached out to draw me to God when I couldn't approach Him on my own.

Now I see how the hand of God was active in my life without me even knowing it. I see it as plain as day now! At first, I couldn't understand how I got from where I was to where I am now. Then I became acquainted with this scripture from Romans 8:26-27: "In the same way the Spirit also helps our weakness; for we do not know how to pray as we should, but the Spirit Himself intercedes for us with groanings too deep for words; and He who searches the hearts knows what the mind of the Spirit is, because He intercedes for the saints according to the will of God."

It's an amazing thing to see how God was with me in those dark, dark times. So back to the original question: how does an addict (or actually, anyone without God in his or her life) develop the right (Godly) priorities?

In order to do this, I had to fall in love with something greater than either myself or my addictions, but I didn't know how to go about it. To fill all the cracks in my life I needed something (which included drugs and alcohol but went far beyond those) – but I had no idea what could possibly fix my predicament.

My world was changed in April 2017 while I was a resident in a rehab facility. I was given a beautiful large-print Bible and glasses by someone who was, and still is, my other very special angel - Ms. Karilyn Tap.

I was a resident in that rehab facility, Aspire, for five months. It became my "cocoon." Ever since the day Ms. Karilyn placed that Bible in my hands, I have never put it down, in a manner of speaking. For four solid months, I read that Bible every single night and wrote in a notebook all the verses that touched me. This became such a priority that I skipped some activities, such as watching TV at night with the other residents, in order to carve out more time with the Lord.

I surrendered my whole life over to the will and care of Father God. On September 25, 2017, I flew out of that rehab facility as a butterfly, a new creation.

I will never be that lost, crippled, addicted person again. Everything has changed and I'll never be the same. I'm now set apart and I've never looked back. I've been adopted into the family of God as His child, a daughter of the Most High. I've been touched by the hand and love of God. All those cracks and holes I mentioned earlier have now been filled. I belong! I'm complete!

Now I have the right priorities. And I have the gifts and promises of God. As 2 Peter 1:1-4 states, "To those who have received a faith of the same kind as ours, by the righteousness of our God and Savior, Jesus Christ: Grace and peace be multiplied to you in the knowledge of God and of Jesus our Lord; seeing that His divine power has granted to us everything pertaining to life and godliness, through the true knowledge of Him who called us by His own glory and excellence. For by these He has granted to us His precious and magnificent promises, so that by them you may become partakers of the divine nature, having escaped the corruption that is in the world by lust."

The heart is the center of our thoughts, our minds, and our decision making (our will). To cultivate the "right priorities" is to love what our God loves, the things that please Him, and to hate what God hates. Direct your heart toward the Lord your God. Romans 12:9 encourages us to "abhor what is evil; cling to what is good."

This attitude will help us conform to the goal of 2 Timothy 3:17: "So that the man of God may be adequate, equipped for every good work." In this, we are rewarded with blessings and favor! And God's favor will change our lives!

With full confidence, I know without a doubt that I'm now on my way to being in sync with God's will and ways. When I stay close to Him, my motives are true and pure, and right doing will eventually be born out of them. Even if we proceed incorrectly at first, we will not go astray permanently as long as we keep the Lord's ways first and foremost on our hearts and minds.

In this present world, nothing will go perfectly 100% of the time, no matter how godly our behavior may be. We will always encounter obstacles; but if our motives are directed by the Lord, we won't be drawn into a situation that's wrong or bad.

Walking closely with the Lord is in a sense like applying a "Christian band-aid" to ungodly situations. The damage resulting from the problem may not be "fixed" right away, but it is on its way to being healed.

"In all your ways acknowledge Him, and He will make your paths straight" (Proverbs 3:6).

"Fear the Lord and turn away from evil. It will be healing to your body and refreshment to your bones" (Proverbs 3:7-8).

The way I hung onto my addiction is now the very same effort by which I hang onto the Lord. I keep Him central and upfront, above everything else.

It wasn't like this in the beginning. It takes time to develop this relationship. But God makes it so easy to fall in love with Him. He has all the qualities each of us lacks in some area of our lives. God's love spreads throughout our brokenness and fills every gap we have. It heals every cut, bruise, scar, and ailment that hinders us.

We eventually come to realize that our attitude is better, and our heart is lighter. Our mind is clearer. We're less angry. We forgive faster. We stop holding onto grudges. We feel more at peace. Problems don't seem as big anymore.

It's as if all the bad, ungodly qualities start melting off us. The shame, anger, unforgiveness, sadness, loneliness, greed, self-centeredness, and so many other things that keep us from true happiness and a close relationship with God our Father, all melt away to the floor. Then God's sunshine comes and dries up all of that mess! He takes it up and away from us.

But listen – all those bad things He takes from us now will be replaced with the fruit of the Spirit, as described in Galatians 5:22-23: "But the fruit of the Spirit is love, joy, peace, patience, kindness, goodness, faithfulness, gentleness, self-control; against such things there is no law."

So, we fall in love with God, realizing we are new creatures in Christ. We want these "right priorities." We won't accept anything less. There is no more room in our spirits for those old fleshly deeds and thoughts. It's similar to putting on new glasses that are the correct prescription. Everything is in focus now. As Jesus said, "Blessed are the pure in heart, for they shall see God" (Matthew 5:8).

"Finally, brethren, whatever is true, whatever is honorable, whatever is right, whatever is pure, whatever is lovely, whatever is of good repute, if there is any excellence and if anything worthy of praise, dwell on these things" (Philippians 4:8).

God creates a pure heart in us and renews us spiritually. This is a process of refreshing and inner cleansing that transforms our hearts.

Once we truly taste the sweetness and goodness of God, we can't help but want to live by the right priorities. There's almost no way we can yearn to go back to the desires of the flesh. And even if we do fall for a moment, we won't want to stay in the corruption of this world.

"Put on the Lord Jesus Christ, and make no provision for the flesh in regard to its lusts" (Romans 13:14).

God helps us by sending us the Comforter, the Holy Spirit. When we pray, He hears our prayers. 1 Peter 3:12 assures us, "For the eyes of the Lord are toward the righteous, and His ears attend to their prayer, but the face of the Lord is against those who do evil."

For me, learning to walk in God was like putting on a new pair of shoes – new to me, and so refreshing! – I, who for so long made every wrong decision, and went down every wrong road.

This has been such a wonderful feeling: becoming a true, upright human being, walking in honor of God, speaking His truths, thinking righteously, feeling wholesome, being in alignment with my Heavenly Father, letting Him direct my paths and words. I can even see the joy I now bring to others! With God's grace, I can get past other people's flaws. I now live by a new set of rules and see His rewards and blessings on my life.

There are so many benefits to having the "right priorities!"

CHAPTER 6

BECOMING COMPLETE

Surrounding Ourselves with Good Things

"And let endurance have its perfect result, so that you may be perfect and complete, lacking in nothing" (James 1:4).

It's said that an apple tree can't produce oranges. Back in my wild days - my Lord, I can still remember - my dad's favorite expression was, "Birds of a feather flock together." And there's another cliché I recall: "You are what you eat."

Love the things that God loves. You should find your joy in activities that are Christlike instead of worldly. 1 John 2:15 instructs believers, "Do not love the world nor the things in the world. If anyone loves the world, the love of the Father is not in him."

When we become Christlike, we will seek things from above. We will want to possess a godly outlook. Jesus said, "Seek first His kingdom and His righteousness, and all these things will be added to you" (Matthew 6:33).

Let's be real. This world is always going to be problematic and violent. 1 John 2:16 says, "For all that is in the world, the lust of the flesh and the lust of the eyes and the boastful pride of life, is not from the Father, but is from the world."

I got caught up in the ways of the world much of my life, until age 53. However, living a Christlike life is what God intended for us from the very beginning – back to the time of Adam and Eve. Coming out of the world's corruption and transitioning to a Christlike life is a journey. We all need other Christians to pull us through to the "other side."

To be successful in this journey, we need to learn about God through His words, determine His characteristics, and take on those characteristics. "By this we know that we have come to know Him, if we keep His commandments" (1 John 2:3).

Not only must we discover His ways and learn them – we must keep His ways, walk in His ways, and speak in conformance with His nature (originating from His life and His love that dwell within us). We conform more and more to His ways, day by day, and this Christlike pattern becomes our new normal as our minds are continually renewed. We are giving birth to new thoughts!

Of course, we're still going to run into problems because we're still living in this sinful world. But now we have a kind of buffer zone – the reality of our new "Christian world." We know we don't have to go through trials alone, because we have built a strong foundation and ideally, we also have an army of fellow Christians helping us mature spiritually.

Even we Christians will continue to have problems within and amongst ourselves, but these can often be dealt with using available "Christian/Biblical apps," such as praying for one another.

We must always keep in mind our chief goal – eternal life with our Creator. As children of God, we realize that these times and this world are only temporary. These things will pass! We must not lose sight of who we now are in Christ. This will help us cope with our burdens in a Christian manner.

"Enter through the narrow gate; for the gate is wide and the way is broad that leads to destruction, and there are many who enter through it" (Matthew 7:13).

We cannot allow this world and our problems to cause us to lose sight of our Christian values. Nothing – no situation – no person – no problem should ever be able to remove us or separate us from who we are in Christ. Listen to what the Apostle Paul said in Romans 8:35, 37-39: "Who will separate us from the love of Christ? Will tribulation, or distress, or persecution, or famine, or nakedness, or peril, or sword?... But in all these things we overwhelmingly conquer through Him who loved us. For I am convinced that neither death, nor life, nor angels, nor principalities, nor things present, nor things to come, nor powers, nor height, nor depth, nor any other created thing, will be able to separate us from the love of God, which is in Christ Jesus our Lord."

During the time I lived in addiction I was so weak. I blew around like a feather here and there, wherever I thought I'd fit in. I often learned that people who I believed loved and cared for me were likewise just filling voids in their lives. I spent forty years aimlessly trying to find myself. My parents loved me— they were not the problem. However, after much time passed, seeing no change in me, they lost respect and gave up on me. Eventually, I also gave up on myself.

Finally, during a time of active addiction and out of desperation, I wrote this poem while I was high:

Please Bring Me Back

Father God,

I feel so scared, tired, and all alone,
All I want to do is come back home.
I put myself and others in harm's way.
I need to run back to Your loving arms and stay.

I love you most,
Your Son Jesus and the Holy Ghost.
I thought I could live life on my own.
I lost my way.
I can't stay.

Please bring me back.
Where I truly belong,
Safe and warm,
Out of this storm.

This is not the way
I thought I would be.
I put myself into this trap.
O, Lord, please bring me back.

After I wrote the poem, I still continued to reach out to anything, in hope of finding something greater than myself.

Then God sent me an "angel." I'm reminded of the scripture found in Hebrews 13:1-2: "Let love of the brethren continue. Do not neglect to show hospitality to strangers, for by this some have entertained angels without knowing it."

In my case, I'm blessed to know some of my angels by name. I'm proud to be able to share the name of one, with her permission – Nancy Martinez from the Hope Team. She swooped down on me like an eagle and picked me up out of my hole. She literally saved my life while I was overdosing. She sat at the hospital with me and cried for me. She stood by me, took me by the ear once again, and placed me in rehab.

This was not my first attempt trying rehab. But on this occasion, it "took." God knew it was time to fulfill my prayer contained in my poem, "Please Bring Me Back." Love you always, Nancy M!

THIS IS YOUR TIME. God's timing is perfect, and any time is the right time for you to invite God into your life and your heart. Now, this moment, is your time! An invitation is extended in Proverbs 3:5-6: "Trust in the Lord with all your heart and do not lean on your own understanding. In all your ways acknowledge Him, and He will make your paths straight."

In the beginning (at least, for me), reading the Word stirred my spirit and opened my mind and heart up to all of God's love and power. It also gave me the hope I was looking for, filled voids I had, and made sense to my mind.

I have to admit, even with all of this, my life still remained unbalanced for a while. My foundation was still unstable. Even though I was moved by reading my Bible, at first I felt its words were just like the words in any other book. But I continued to read and surround myself with God-minded people.

At this time, I still had one foot in my old world, because that's all I knew – its false comfort and its people who seemed to fill that hole I had. Somehow, I knew there had to be more… something better…because I still ended up with the same problems.

As teenagers, we think we know it all. And as for me, later in life I said wow, I wish I had taken school more seriously and spent less time fooling around. I wish I had listened to my parents more and had been more disciplined. Etc., etc.

Well, I've learned that becoming a Christian doesn't mean you immediately know everything there is to know. But the Holy Spirit lives within us to help us grow up spiritually. As I continue my journey with the Lord, I see the Spirit teaching me as I go. And our Lord desires that ALL believers "grow in the grace and knowledge of our Lord and Savior Jesus Christ" (2 Peter 3:18).

The Holy Spirit helps us mature and stretch as we travel along this road. We should feel comfortable and at ease, providing we continue to walk in the path that God has laid out for us. The stubbornness of our egos will start to diminish. Our selfish wants will become less and less important. Others' feelings become of greater significance as we begin to perceive we're not the only ones in this world who have needs.

In Matthew 6:25-26, 31-32, Jesus taught His followers, "'For this reason I say to you, do not be worried about your life…Is not life more than food?…Look at the birds of the air, that they do not sow, nor reap nor gather into barns, and yet your heavenly Father feeds them. Are you not worth much more than they? Do not worry then…for your heavenly Father knows that you need all these things…'"

Once we begin to realize that Father God is taking care of our needs, gratefulness and an attitude of thanksgiving come into play. Our hearts will yearn to live even closer to God, learning more and more of His ways – knowing that His ways are better and higher than ours.

"'For My thoughts are not your thoughts, nor are your ways My ways,' declares the Lord. 'For as the heavens are higher than the earth, so are My ways higher than your ways and My thoughts than your thoughts'" (Isaiah 55:8-9).

It helps me to look at life like this: I'm sitting in a room surrounded by solid walls. Now, I don't see what's on the other side, but God does! So, am I going to trust what I think is going on in the other room, or do I trust God and wait on Him?

I have chosen to follow God's direction for my life as well as in all my decision making. And ever since I made this choice (2.5 years as of this writing), I'm so amazed, as well as others around me, watching Him bestow blessing after blessing.

Now listen! Life is life. It's not always going to be wonderful. But when we make godly decisions, our circumstances can't get worse in the long run. In time, the situation - whatever it is - will pass without our experiencing worldly regrets or heartache. Amen!

"Therefore…let us press on to maturity" (Hebrews 6:1).

"Until we all attain to the unity of the faith, and of the knowledge of the Son of God, to a mature man, to the measure of the stature which belongs to the fullness of Christ…we are no longer to be children, tossed here and there by waves and carried about by every wind of doctrine" (Ephesians 4:13-14).

CHAPTER 7

WALKING IN THE SPIRIT OF GOD

PART 1 – FINDING OUR PURPOSE

Our goal should be this: to stop living for ourselves and instead, to live for something far more important - God's purposes. This means coming to a place in our lives where we "transfer" ourselves to living in His Spirit. We're totally surrendered to God's will.

Before I knew the Lord, my mom once told me, "You're the most selfish person I ever knew." You know, that still hurts me to this day – because she was right! My God, she was right! I make it up to her now by loving God and keeping His commandments. God rest her soul, if she's looking down on me, I can finally make her heart glad!

As we grow in the faith, losing sight of ourselves becomes the norm. We no longer cater to the old selfish motives. Our new highest priority is to live godly. I myself now feel more comfortable living for God than for myself!

This is what it means to die to our old selves. Our old ways of thinking and feeling no longer exist. Living a "me first" life brings no joy anymore. It's now become ugly, unsatisfying, and boring!

Walking in God's Spirit is like walking through a wall. We leave behind our old fleshly life that's all about me, me, me, what's best for me.

Walking increasingly closer to God is also like a snake losing its skin. We should be shedding our old selves as we bathe in, listen to, study, walk in, and think about God's words and ways – building His kingdom and sowing godly seed.

By keeping to God's path, before we know it, we will reach a new spiritual plateau or realm. We enter into the light of the Lord, walking by faith and not by sight (2 Corinthians 5:7). We've been touched by the Spirit of God and we have a new, exciting existence. This is an amazing feeling! Looking inside ourselves, we are developing the very heart of God. We have found our new home as part of His family and we should never want to turn back to our old ways. As written in 1 Corinthians 6:17, "The one who joins himself to the Lord is one spirit with Him."

As for myself, God's values are now more important to me than those I formerly held. Well, to be honest, my values have actually become His values. As someone who has now experienced God's favor and all His blessings, I find myself in a totally new skin – a new person with a new character and new friends.

So, I asked myself, now what? Maybe this sounds crazy to you, but I paused and asked God, "Okay, You shaped me and You molded me. I love you! But what do You want me to do? I feel all dressed up, but with nowhere to go!" To be completely honest, it was frustrating. I started pleading with God, "Please,

please, show me my purpose now! You've blessed me with a home and a car. My health is improving. I don't want all this for nothing. I want to do Your will!" I didn't understand why I wasn't "saving the world."

Finally, I've learned my true purpose. It's not to have spiritual "Popeye" muscles. God wants each believer to simply shine His love and grace to others who need Him!

"Therefore, my beloved brethren, be steadfast, immovable, always abounding in the work of the Lord, knowing that your toil is not in vain in the Lord" (1 Corinthians 15:58).

I discovered that all I have to do is be ME, the person God created me to be! When I came to the knowledge of God and made His ways my ways, I found my true purpose and identity in God. I must allow God's light to shine through my own life consistently so I can serve as an example to others.

"For we have become partakers of Christ, if we hold fast the beginning of our assurance firm until the end" (Hebrews 3:14).

I've learned I don't have to be a big, powerful superhero. I just humble myself and show God's truths through my life. As believers, we should be walking billboards for the Lord, with our actions attracting others to Him.

Or in the words of Jesus: "Let your light shine before men in such a way that they may see your good works, and glorify your Father who is in heaven" (Matthew 5:16).

PART 2 – THINGS CHANGE

I still remember my "pre-God" attitudes and actions. In the past, it was my practice to hold onto and nurse my grudges and complaints. Sometimes I even planned my revenge and carried out paybacks. I felt this strategy made things right and even helped me feel better. Hurting someone else was like placing a band-aid on my wounds.

Now I'm sure many of you can relate to at least some of this. And all for what?

Even back then, I was aware that the Bible contained words like "'Vengeance is Mine,' says the Lord" (Romans 12:19). See, even I knew some of the Bible! But living in the world as I did, I wanted worldly results, instant gratification.

Now I am becoming more grateful each day. The person I used to be was truly awful and so wrong on so many levels. Each day reveals that a new "God" quality is being instilled in me. For example, one night not long ago a dear friend needed a ride home from the hospital. However, I was caught up in watching a very good movie. To be honest, I still had a bit of my former self-centered attitude. I almost made up an excuse, just as the "old me" would have. But I didn't!

To my surprise, very quickly I felt the love I had for my friend and asked God for forgiveness. This all happened in less than a minute. Looking back at the end of the night, I was pleased that I chose to serve my Lord.

I am grateful that God is now placing me in these types of situations and that He enables me to serve Him by serving others. I am thankful that He gave me a changed heart. Pleasing God is so much more important to me than watching even a very, very good movie!

Jesus tells us in Matthew 25:40, "Truly I say to you, to the extent that you did it to one of these brothers of Mine, even the least of them, you did it to Me." And in Philippians 2:4, the Apostle Paul instructs us, "Do not merely look out for your own personal interests, but also for the interests of others."

Sometimes I start losing sight of who I am in Christ. Yes, I still have "off days" and begin to lose touch with God. It's a very dark place for me - as if I were in a hole - a sickening feeling, like a death sentence. Fortunately, this is an increasingly rare occurrence! But it does happen since we live in the world, and at times we are going to be touched by its elements. 1 John 5:19 warns us, "The whole world lies in the power of the evil one."

During those times I remember that for decades I lived in that dark world on purpose. But now I can't handle it anymore, even for five minutes.

Jesus said, "These things I have spoken to you, so that in Me you may have peace. In the world you have tribulation, but take courage; I have overcome the world" (John 16:33).

And He has given me courage! Although God is Spirit, His Holy Spirit wants to fill our entire being with the earthly purpose He has in mind for each of us. When we're filled with God's Holy Spirit, we know who to run back to when we become sidetracked or are attacked by this world. We no longer have to sit alone in our sickness. We are only one praise away from getting back to our true home – where our hearts now live, in God Almighty!

PART 3 – INTUITION

Believers who keep godly company and stay pure in heart and motives are like spiritual magnets - clinging to and staying connected to God.

All people possess some degree of intuition that, when properly operating within the soul, alerts us when we're in harm's way. In such instances, a person with a functional soul will be motivated to respond appropriately.

When the Holy Spirit of God comes to dwell within us, the spirits of unbelievers (those not connected to the Lord) will recognize His presence. If we are sensitive to the Holy Spirit, He will protect us from those who are living in defiance of God. Having the Holy Spirit within us actually wards off such people and they will tend to move further and further away from us. The worldly spirits within them will become conflicted and will not want to remain around us.

This was my personal experience when I was on the "other side of the wall," which I mentioned in a previous chapter. I remember why I couldn't be around people of God. I was stopped by my shame of knowing I wasn't doing right. I wanted what the Christians had, but I wasn't ready to give up the beliefs and activities I thought made me happy. Now, as a believer, I have learned that some people may never even try to find God in this life.

Since we are still "in the flesh" we can't always see the spiritual dangers surrounding us. The Holy Spirit may guide our intuition by compelling us to move away from certain people or situations. It reminds me of a cat that senses immediate danger somewhere in the mist. The hair on the back of its neck may stand up. It may hiss, growl, or arch its back.

Since the devil is a liar, he's always trying to trick us. He makes sin seem appealing and attempts to stir up the lusts of our flesh, tempting us with earthly desires to lure us into his pit. As 1 Peter 5:8 describes it, "Be of sober spirit, be on the alert. Your adversary, the devil, prowls around like a roaring lion, seeking someone to devour."

But thanks be to God, He has equipped us in every way! "The Lord will protect you from all evil; He will keep your soul. The Lord will guard your going out and your coming in from this time forth and forever" (Psalm 121:7-8).

I'm certain you've heard these expressions many times: "Trust your intuition." "Trust your gut feeling." For those of us who are connected to God and rely on His Holy Spirit, we can trust Him to guide us in many ways, one being our intuition.

CHAPTER 8

WELCOME HOME

When we come to the Lord and know this is truly where we belong, we are home – home with the Lord in this life, and in the life hereafter. We've always belonged to the Lord, but now we know we do!

"I have redeemed you; I have called you by name; you are Mine!" (Isaiah 43:1).

"For if we live, we live for the Lord, or if we die, we die for the Lord; therefore whether we live or die, we are the Lord's" (Romans 14:8).

Now that we have come to know our true place in life we should act accordingly. We do this with open arms. This is not a chore or a burden. As the Apostle Paul wrote, "I thank Christ Jesus our Lord, who has strengthened me, because He considered me faithful, putting me into service" (1 Timothy 1:12).

Serving God will bring many benefits and rewards for our lives. Not only does it please God when we do right, but anyone with whom we associate will benefit from our kind words, good deeds, and godly example. According to Proverbs 3:6, serving the Lord will cause us to receive His direction for our own lives. "In all your ways acknowledge Him, and He will make your paths straight."

By the time I gave my life to God, most of my friends had already passed away. Had that not been the case, I would have tried to show them the way to God. If they had failed to respond, I would have had to distance myself from them.

In the beginning, starting my life over, I was very lonely trying to develop friendships with new people who had healthy lifestyles and a love for God. Although I was still uncomfortable at times, I knew the feeling would eventually pass. I wanted what they had…God…and I wasn't going to accept anything less. I wasn't going to turn around and go back. I knew that the old life was over and dead to me.

So, I trusted God and let Him lead me, and to my surprise…I belong! I'm going on three years now and I have the right people in my life. I have a beautiful church, Faith Assembly, with its pastor Carl Stephens. I now volunteer at the same rehab facility where I dedicated my life to God and am part of a monthly support group for its graduates. I participate in a weekly prayer group and attend many activities with my new friends. We're family!

I did experience some of this with my old "family" in the homeless camp, but in such a different way. We all lived ungodly lives and reaped the repercussions. With the exception of myself and one other, all lost their lives. As far as my biological family was concerned, I was truly the black sheep, a total disgrace in every way imaginable.

I have to say I am so grateful that God showed me favor and even gave me the opportunity to write this book. I am home, and I would like to take you home also to our Father

God. WELCOME HOME! This is where we belong.

As John, one of Jesus' disciples, put it: "See how great a love the Father has bestowed on us, that we would be called children of God; and such we are. For this reason the world does not know us, because it did not know Him" (1 John 3:1). But we know Him, and He knows us!

The greatest gift we can receive is to know who we are – children of the Most High. It's our responsibility to show others who they are in Him. Jesus said, "Enter through the narrow gate; for the gate is wide and the way is broad that leads to destruction, and there are many who enter through it" (Matthew 7:14).

We are the few. And even with the lifestyle I lived, I'm saved and forgiven! My purpose for writing this book is this: I took, and led, many people down the wrong road. My prayer is that by writing this book, I will now lead many up the right road. I'm very thankful and blessed! In just the short time I've been serving God, I've also been forgiven by most of my family, including my children!

It's a wonderful feeling when we are able to connect with God's children in a world that's so cruel and harsh. We can also obtain perfect harmony, joy, and peace knowing that our God is in complete control. He always finds a way for us. Proverbs 3:5 encourages us, "Trust in the LORD with all your heart and do not lean on your own understanding."

When we come together with other members of God's family, all seeking to have God's intentions first and foremost, God's Spirit is among us. "We will know by this that we are of the truth, and will assure our heart before Him" (1 John 3:19).

It's never too late to be forgiven by God Almighty. The same opportunity is available to everyone. Just read the story of the prodigal son in the Bible! The Lord will lead you in the everlasting way (Psalm 139:24).

CHAPTER 9

BEING OBEDIENT

OBEDIENCE – wow, what a word! People have many different outlooks and feelings about this word. Many even removed it from their marriage vows.

Obedience to sources other than those designated by God can result in damage to, or loss of, our self-respect, which is a basic human need. We all have a desire to be respected by others, as well, since we were created in God's image. When we grant our obedience to an authority not designated by God, we may feel that we're somehow less than God sees us - very small or inadequate. From my old life, I remember a former boyfriend who was set off by the smallest things. All hell would break loose if I didn't do something his way. His responses would make me shake and cry.

Sometimes legitimate authorities established by the Lord (such as supervisors, teachers, government representatives, etc.) elevate their authority to improper levels. Possibly a promotion goes to their heads, or their need to feel superior

NEW!

causes them to misuse their leadership positions to build their own egos.

In either case, it's normal for us to resent those who demand obedience and then use their authority to degrade or outrightly abuse us. As a result, the word "obedience" takes on a controversial meaning for many people.

But…our God requires our obedience. Listen to what His Word says.

Jesus says in the Gospel of John 15:14: "You are My friends if you do what I command you" and again in John 14:15: "If you love Me, you will keep My commandments."

The Bible even says we will be blessed if we obey Him! Deuteronomy 5:33 tells us, "You shall walk in all the way which the Lord your God has commanded you, that you may live and that it may be well with you, and that you may prolong your days in the land which you will possess." And Jesus tells us, "…blessed are those who hear the word of God and observe it" (Luke 11:28).

The bottom line is a trust issue. How do I (or anyone, for that matter) put trust in someone or something I can't touch, see, or hear? We live in a physical world and experience it through our five senses – by hearing, tasting, smelling, touching, and seeing. We expect to see tangible results. Most of us operate as "here and now" people. We want what we want now!

It's hard enough as it is to totally trust (put our faith into) people, organizations, and other physical things. Many of us feel we can only trust and rely on ourselves. And then, someone brings up God – Someone we can't see, taste, smell, touch, or hear audibly! And yet, God wants more for us than we ever imagined – grand things.

From my own perspective, I have sat on every side of every fence. At one time, my desires were not in line with God's will at all. I now see why I had so much trouble, grief, and sadness in my life. My life before I knew God was always in doubt: "So your life shall hang in doubt before you; and you will be in dread night and day, and shall have no assurance of your life" (Deuteronomy 28:66).

Now, Satan, who is a liar, makes the world and all its lusts look more attractive than they really are. They're NOT! I'm here to tell you from personal experience. I am qualified to speak on this subject with all the knowledge that came from living every which way. It's all deceit – all a lie. Only living on God's side of the fence will bring the life-saving truth that provides us with His knowledge and wisdom! The grass is only green all the time on the Lord's side! After I started my journey with God, things I previously thought I wanted now seemed petty.

When I first began attending a church service at the residential drug rehab center, I didn't know where to start. I had come to a place where I'd become really real with myself. I had tried all else, pretty much been everywhere, and done everything. But when I began reading my Bible, the door I sought for about 54 years OPENED. I walked through it and never looked back! I found that without God, I would never be whole.

Jesus says to all of us, "I am the way, and the truth, and the life; no one comes to the Father but through Me" (John 14:6).

I asked the Holy Spirit to come into my heart, and He took up residency. I, in turn, took up residence in Him. "For I am convinced that neither death, nor life, nor angels, nor principalities, nor things present, nor things to come, nor powers, nor height, nor depth, nor any other created thing, will be able to separate us from the love of God, which is in Christ Jesus our Lord" (Romans 8:38-39).

I no longer doubted. I gave God my all: all my trust, all my faith, all my life, all my love, all my dedication, all my direction – and all my obedience. And the Holy Spirit began teaching me: "The Helper, the Holy Spirit, whom the Father will send in My name, He will teach you all things, and bring to your remembrance all that I said to you" (John 14:26).

This is the best decision I've ever made, and there's no going back. There's absolutely nothing to go back to! When you accept God into your life it's like every "hole" gets filled.

For the believer to establish a lasting trust in Christ (especially a new believer) it is imperative to set aside all materialistic "stuff," our own egos, and the opinions of others. We must turn off the distractions of the world that block out the Spirit of God, shutting down the worldly influences as we would turn off the TV. As for myself, I began to remove everything in my life that would hinder and rob me of a strong relationship with God.

We believers have already received the gift of the Holy Spirit. Understand that He's there, He's alive, He's within you! When we spend time alone with the Lord, we will start to feel the uplifting power of the Holy Spirit come alive in us, working deep within us. "You are from God, little children, and have overcome them; because greater is He who is in you than he who is in the world" (1 John 4:4).

Once we have truly surrendered our lives to the Lord, we will discover that obedience is no longer a problem. In fact, obeying our Father God is an honor! And when we honor and obey God, we in turn are honoring our family, our spouses, our friends and co-workers, and ourselves.

We obey a God who sees us as the light of the world, and a city set on a hill that cannot be hidden (Matthew 5:14). In God's eyes, we're His jewels and the salt of the earth! Even in my marriages I never had anyone tell me such loving things (although I did my best to respect my spouses).

Therefore, why would it be difficult to submit to a God

who genuinely loves us, inside and out - more than any human relationship we may experience on earth? Our heavenly Father forgives us of all our mistakes and lifts us up when we are downtrodden. Let us celebrate our obedience to our Lord with worship, honor, respect, regard, praise, joy, trust, tribute, admiration, goodness, delight, and devotion!

Psalm 37:4 provides this assurance: "Delight yourself in the LORD; and He will give you the desires of your heart." I know for myself, I want to be obedient to my Father in heaven. Adopting God's values as our own is the best assurance we can give ourselves to have very blessed lives - lives full of joy, peace, and all the spiritual fruit such a life bears. In my case, God is restoring and mending the important relationships I had lost due to my addiction. This couldn't have happened without God softening their hearts toward me.

The bottom line is that I have decided to love and be obedient to our Lord God - the One who loves me, created me, and wants only good things for me. My Father God is the One I choose.

"I, JoAnne Ranucci, take Thee, the Lord God Almighty, to be my God and Savior, to love and to cherish, to obey till the eternal life which awaits me according to God's holy ordinance. To Thee I pledge my faith and myself, my very being, unto You always. Amen!"

You, the reader, are welcome to use my statement of commitment as a template to develop your own vow.

CHAPTER 10

HIGHER LEVELS

The Lord guides us to new levels in our Christian walk with Him. As we mature in God's ways, He will give us different assignments. He puts various individuals in our path for us to help and bless. We are God's hands. In serving others, we serve Him (Matthew 25:40).

As we closely and steadily walk with God, He gives us what we need in order to accomplish what He desires us to do or be for others, depending upon the particular situation. Every season brings its own challenges, and our job is to remain faithful and attentive. We are like pieces in His puzzle that he continually moves around. He trusts us to complete new tasks as they arise. He may adjust our roles depending upon what He wants us to do for Him. We reach out to others as His disciples, His soldiers, His teachers, His listeners, His coaches, His mentors, His sponsors, His friends, His mothers, fathers, brothers, and sisters as the need arises. We are to attract people to our Father God!

Not too long ago I was a lost, broken, and empty vessel. With the help of one of God's seasoned disciples, I was taught and nurtured in the ways of God. Now, in turn, I have become a disciple who is able to nurture and disciple others with the goal of helping lead them to God. It's like adding links to a chain.

The Lord will give us assignments throughout our lives. In these assignments, God will equip us with what we need to carry out His will. He also protects us as we serve: "He will give His angels charge concerning you, to guard you in all your ways" (Psalm 91:11).

In addition, the Lord provides strength and courage and causes our fears to subside. Philippians 4:13 assures us that we can do everything through Him who gives us strength.

In order for us to achieve higher levels in our Christian walk and to please God, we must have faith. In fact, the Book of Hebrews 11:6 tells us that without faith, it is impossible to please God!

Operating by faith can be a scary thing because it's like walking along a path wearing blinders over our eyes! But when we consistently strive for this goal of walking by faith instead of by sight, we are truly God's disciples. The more we reach beyond the flesh that used to limit us, the more we proclaim our confidence in our Father God. "Then you will walk in your way securely and your foot will not stumble" (Proverbs 3:23).

As God directs us in His wisdom and His ways, giving us the courage to carry out His will, we will keep on climbing to new levels in our faith. We will enjoy pleasing Him daily. Our focus begins to revolve around giving our Father joy and obedience in our thoughts, our hearts, our actions, and our words – in fact, with our total lives.

We reach a place where we see God for who He truly is: our Refuge, our Strength, our Father and Creator, our Protector, our Teacher, and our Salvation. And we know that He has chosen us! He knew us before we were even conceived! Listen to the words of the prophet proclaiming God's Word in Jeremiah 1:5: "Before I formed you in the womb I knew you, and before you were born I consecrated you."

We need to truly believe that we are created, loved, and wanted by our loving, kind, awesome Father God. Once we grab hold of this we will (with full confidence) thrive, flourish, increase, and blossom in each and every level to which God takes us. We are God's treasures! Trust Him to place you where you need to be.

"He made from one man every nation of mankind to live on all the face of the earth, having determined their appointed times and the boundaries of their habitation" (Acts 17:26).

So, understand this: If we walk with God we will be exactly where we need to be. He will place people in our path to whom we can minister and guide in His direction. We can now teach others what we have learned, letting them know that God has given His Son to provide us a way to salvation, an escape from sin! Our lives will demonstrate that, although this world has its troubles, we do not have to conform to it - but rather be transformed by the renewing of our minds (Romans 12:2).

The Holy Spirit will work through us to reveal Himself to others, guiding and shaping their hearts and minds so that they may also seek and find God, and allow the Spirit to come alive in them. We get to witness and share about God's miracles; we have a clear path, a good conscience, and a godly confidence to direct others to His truths.

Our spiritual growth levels are endless and countless, allowing us to perform continuous, unlimited, and uninhibited works for God. We are His soldiers!

"The things which you have heard from me in the presence

of many witnesses, entrust these to faithful men who will be able to teach others also. Suffer hardship with me, as a good soldier of Christ Jesus" (2 Timothy 2:2-3).

Living the Christian life is not boring! It's the highest level we can achieve in this life – coming to the knowledge of who we really are and from whom we came – carrying out the will of our Father Creator. This is, and always will be, the biggest and most important accomplishment we can claim for ourselves and share with others. This is our TRUE mission because, when all is said and done, what's really left other than our eternal life with our God?

Therefore, in this temporary phase of life, I encourage you to strive for the highest level – finding God, telling others about Him, leading people to Him – living by faith and not by sight. Love and honor God with all that you are and all that you have. You will be blessed. You will be favored. You will be set apart.

"Blessed is a man who perseveres under trial; for once he has been approved, he will receive the crown of life which the Lord has promised to those who love Him" (James 1:12).

CHAPTER 11
FORGIVENESS

PART 1 – FORGIVING OTHERS

I'm not going to lie. Being a Christian is hard. We don't just float around on a God cloud all day. It's tough. You have to hold your tongue when someone rubs you the wrong way. You need to be nonjudgmental. You need to see even the worst of people through the eyes of God. NOT EASY AT ALL!

Most of us eventually come to a place of discovering what makes our lives go round. I have discovered that the benefits of following the Lord are overwhelming. And the benefits of loving God and having a relationship with Him are permanent, concrete, consistent, and never changing.

Yes, there will still be times we want to SCREAM at the top of our lungs and tell someone off! But we don't. Instead, we embrace our love-relationship with God and know that He is in control. We honor and respect His commandments. When we come back to our reliance on Him, our joy and peace return to us. When we stand on our relationship with God, we are standing on firm ground!

Remember that we cannot pick and choose which commandments we will obey. If we sin by breaking one, we've sinned in ALL. As the Book of James 2:10 says, "For whoever keeps the whole law and yet stumbles in one point, he has become guilty of all." As Christians, we know we need to forgive. In fact, we are commanded to forgive! As I said, God's commandments are not optional.

At one time I, like many others, couldn't comprehend the healing power of forgiveness. It is a true healer! So how do we, as people of flesh and egos, deal with hurt and pain? How do we learn to "let go" and not hold grudges? When we truly study the teachings of the New Testament, we will see that God understands our dilemma. The Bible helps us discover the very heart of God, reminding us of what Christ has done for us.

The Lord says it is to our own benefit to let go of not just some, but all of our pain and hurt. We benefit more than those whom we choose to forgive! 1 Peter 5:7 provides reassurance: "Casting all your anxiety on Him, because He cares for you." Jesus' love for us is so profound. He knows that letting go of something done to us by another is important; He wants us to be well in mind and spirit.

Jesus is well aware of the traps set up for us by Satan. One such trap is the idea that it's okay to hold onto unforgiveness. Think of what a bear trap would do to you if you stepped into it. Similarly, continued unforgiveness puts a spiritual "hold" on us that will lead us into more sin. We continue to build up resentment. We lose our focus on the Lord and our Christian walk, our conduct, will operate at less than 100%.

The Holy Spirit will bring to our attention those whom we need to forgive. And we surely need God's grace, the help of the

Holy Spirit, to extend that forgiveness to others! When Christ takes root in our hearts, we will be able to feel His love and compassion so as to grant them mercy. Our Lord Jesus knows that forgiveness is one of the keys to our all-around well-being.

When we obey in this matter we continue on with a good conscience and a light heart. Our joy and peace will surely return! The "bear trap" opens up and we are able to walk freely out of the lion's den. And that pleases our Lord Jesus! He desires that we remain free of Satan's tricks and lies.

At one time, I, like many others, couldn't comprehend that forgiveness is a real healer - one that will never cause additional mayhem. In fact, it's like setting up a stop sign to mayhem! Or putting out a fire.

Unforgiveness is the ingredient that keeps the flames growing and flaring up out of control. These flames then lead to resentment, anger, irritation, distress, outrage, grief, etc., etc. The conflagration spreads and much destruction results. Sometimes it's so painful that we can't seem to get past it.

Forgiveness, on the other hand, is like a pail of water or a fire extinguisher that puts out the flames. In the national news, I actually saw an example of Jesus' spirit of forgiveness in action. A female police officer had gone into the wrong apartment and killed an innocent man with her gun, claiming she thought he had broken into her apartment! When she later was convicted of murder, the brother of the slain man took the stand. He said he could forgive the policewoman for shooting his brother and hoped she would give her life to Christ!

Unforgiveness is like a prison sentence. Forgiveness is the key to obtaining your freedom, although it may not seem like it! You may be so upset that you can't see past the fog. But I can assure you that forgiveness clears that fog, and all you see and feel is the wonder of the love of God. He will comfort you and help you move past it.

The following scripture applies to many situations, including unforgiveness: "Trust in the LORD with all your heart and do not lean on your own understanding" (Proverbs 3:5).

Although we live physically in the flesh, God has given us His Spirit. For this reason, believers are capable of walking in the power of the Spirit that works within us, as mentioned in Ephesians 3:20. The power to forgive is a God-given ability and one that will help you retain and restore your joy, your freedom, your good conscience, and your relationship with God.

The act of extending forgiveness is very powerful. Not many will understand this, and people may even criticize you for doing it. But you have to live in your own skin and work toward maintaining a clear, clean conscience. It's not your responsibility to please other people. It IS your responsibility to be in a good, right standing with God Almighty. Do you love your God? Then step up with the help of the Holy Spirit and rise above Satan's traps and others' opinions.

This is between you and your Father in heaven.

Forgive, and you will develop deeper roots in your relationship with God.

Forgive, and you will build a stronger foundation.

Forgive, and you will become more balanced.

Forgive, and you will gain more wisdom.

Forgive, and you will maintain a good state of mind.

Forgive, and you will learn to have the right priorities.

Forgive, and you will become complete in Christ.

Forgive, and you will more consistently walk in the Spirit of God.

Forgive, and you will know you're at home in God's loving arms.

Forgive, and you will be blessed for your obedience.

Forgive, and you will move into higher spiritual levels.

Forgive, and you will become a testimony of God's grace.

PART 2 – FORGIVING OURSELVES

Yes, forgiving ourselves is sometimes harder than we think. We can't just jump out of our own skin and thoughts. We need to find ways to cope with our mistakes using a variety of remedies and techniques. Some of us will have to work through a lot of guilt and shame because of the hurt and destruction we caused. We may have many regrets. This is not easy! I still deal with these issues. It's a form of PTSD (post-traumatic stress disorder). And when these past events resurface to affect our present mind, they cause a recurrence of grief, hurt, and pain.

Although we are now living Christian lives, Satan doesn't want to ever let go. He will remind us of past sins, using our previous indiscretions to try to bring us back down to those demeaning levels where we once lived. These thoughts can be triggered at any given time by various memories, such as a song, a scent, a physical location, etc.

Unforgiveness creates many obstacles for developing the relationship we need with God.
"Be kind to one another, tender-hearted, forgiving each other, Just as God In Christ also has forgiven you" (Ephesians 4:32).

So…where do we start? Well, at the beginning. The Gospel of John 3:16 assures us, "God so loved the world, that He gave His only begotten Son, that whoever believes in Him shall not perish, but have eternal life." Father God gave His one and only Son because He knew we would need forgiveness. Let this be some healing to your soul! Likewise, Psalm 103:12 says, "As far as the east is from the west, so far has He removed our transgressions from us."

Now that we know without a doubt that God forgives us, let's work on us. We, in turn, must do good from here on out. We also have to get over ourselves. We've been beaten up enough that we've sustained many wounds. Let's stop adding to them!

It's a new mindset or heart condition that we finally accept what we did wrong and use it to benefit others. We can now grab someone else's hand and pull them out of that same "muck" where we used to be "stuck."

PTSD goes so deep that some will need the help of medication or counseling. Earlier I mentioned techniques and remedies that helped me in this area when at one point the memories of my past wouldn't stop plaguing me. Even though I was saved, born again, I was suffering and being tormented. It actually became so bad that I couldn't take it anymore and needed a way out.

Even then, I knew I was never returning to my addiction (which is what Satan wanted me to do). It was not an option anymore! So, to release the valve on this rising steam, to receive some kind of relief from the pressure of my past thoughts, I died! Yes! I gave my "old self" a funeral. In my mind, I took a shoebox, dug a hole six feet deep, put my old, broken self into the shoebox, gave myself last rites, and buried myself with all my past regrets.

This worked well for a while, but I discovered that it was

not a permanent solution. So, I came up with a quick way to rid myself of these horrible old thoughts that tried to stunt my spiritual growth, rip me apart, tear me down, and hold me hostage.

I imagined a small box which I held in my hand. Into this box I immediately placed every bothersome thought. Then I blew it, as one would blow a feather, upward to God. As I did this I would say, "God, I don't own this thought or behavior any longer. It's not mine. I give it to You. I'm healed in the name of Jesus. I am a child of God, now and always."

So, these are a couple of my ideas. You may develop some of your own.

Forgive yourself! Because:

"If anyone is in Christ, he is a new creature; the old things passed away; behold, new things have come" (2 Corinthians 5:17).

"There is now no condemnation for those who are in Christ Jesus" (Romans 8:1).

Be good to yourself. Be kind to yourself. You deserve to have joy, love, peace, and harmony in your life.

CHAPTER 12

BE GOD'S TESTIMONY

The Great Commission

"Go therefore and make disciples of all the nations, baptizing them in the name of the Father and the Son and the Holy Spirit, teaching them to observe all that I commanded you" (Matthew 28:19-20).

It's hard to hold back all of what the Holy Spirit has revealed to you. When you first trust in Jesus and the Holy Spirit (the Comforter) has occupied your soul, it's out of your control – you must share all His wisdom and truth. Demonstrating the fruit of the Spirit to others is compulsory (Galatians 5:22-23)!

The best way for me to explain it is this: Say you have been living all your life in a cave, doing "cave things," only knowing "cave life." The cave represents all the shameful, sinful things you did in darkness: adultery, murder, dishonesty, and anything else that goes against the ways of God.

Then one day the rock you were polishing comes loose and breaks away and suddenly you see a tiny light. You become curious and start breaking away more of the stones of your cave. You don't want rocks preventing you from seeing more and more of this light, so you keep chipping away.

Finally, you step out of your cave for the first time. Coming out of the cave is where you find conviction of those sinful actions and behaviors. The Holy Spirit then enters into your being and soul. That was the light you were seeing and sensing as you were chipping away at the cave rocks. Now, with the Holy Spirit inside you, you are amazed by all this beauty and wonder! You see the sun, some wispy clouds, the colors of the flowers, trees, and grass, perhaps some pools of water or rolling hills, and on and on.

Would you not tell your friends back in the cave about this miraculous discovery? No! You would be screaming at the top of your lungs, calling everyone you've known and loved all your life to come and see the light. Right?!

You can't keep this knowledge to yourself. It's too much for you to keep inside yourself and not share! You feel an overwhelming desire to tell and show others.

Well, it's the same thing with God's Word! Your new knowledge has to be shared, given away freely. Not only do we inherit God's favor and blessing in this lifetime, but we are convinced of our eternal life in His Son as stated in 1 John 5:11.

This is major! The Bible teaches us to "proclaim good tidings of His salvation from day to day. Tell of His glory among the nations, His wonderful deeds among all the peoples" (Psalm 96:2-3).

I found this out before it was too late, praise God! It boils down to this: The primary purpose for everyone here on this earth is to find the One True God…to praise and worship our

Lord...and to lead others to Him. This world can be ugly, but even so, we believers can live in joy, peace, and love under any circumstances.

We also yearn to live right by God's standards. We have been made wholesome in His sight, upright, set apart. We know without a doubt that we are greatly valued by God Himself. After all, we were created by The Great I Am, who bestowed us with gifts and powers! And when we feel valued, we, in turn, want others to know they're equally as important to Him. We love others because we ourselves are loved. We forgive others because we ourselves have been forgiven.

We must be beacons that shine in the dark. We are to be pure light that will lead people home to Father God. Our main responsibility is to develop and give away what we know of God's truth. In 2 Timothy 1:8-9, the Apostle Paul urges believers, "Do not be ashamed of the testimony of our Lord...who has saved us and called us with a holy calling."

I want to finish this book by quoting the words of Jesus our Lord written in the Gospel of Matthew 5:14-16: "You are the light of the world. A city set on a hill cannot be hidden; nor does anyone light a lamp and put it under a basket, but on the lampstand, and it gives light to all who are in the house. Let your light shine before men in such a way that they may see your good works, and glorify your Father who is in heaven."

I was lost and now I'm found. My prayer is for you to also be filled with God's Holy Spirit and to truly know that you are a child of the Most High God...that you have eternal life...and that you have the ability to bring others to God through this great knowledge. Don't keep it inside - give it away.

May God bless you all.

P.S. I love you, Daddy Larry!

CONTENTS

1

THE BIG BEGINNING

Much of what you will read in this book is true. It actually happened one very hot summer, not long ago. And, every single character in this book is a real, living, ordinary person, just like you and me. Their actions may seem ordinary to some, but to those of us who love construction, what they do is extraordinary. And, if you follow your interests with your head and your heart, something extraordinary can happen to you, too. We begin our story with Sam, a typical young boy who was about begin an extraordinary adventure and discover his calling.

Sam ran to the front door with thundering feet and flung it wide open with a bang. What was that loud rumbling noise? Errrra, Errrra, RRRRRRR, VRRRR. It sounded like big machines; he was sure of it. Errrra, ERRA. It sounded, to Sam, like a rumbling, roaring machine was saying, "I love to work." Sam thought to himself, "I love to work, too."

"Mom, it's starting!" he yelled back to Mom in the house. "Mr. O'Hara was right! It's starting!" His parents' friend, Mr. O'Hara, was the manager of their neighborhood borough. Sam remembered Mr. O'Hara telling him about a new construction project.

"Sam, an enormous construction crew will be working in our neighborhood this summer digging up the roads to replace old gas lines." Right here in Sam's neighborhood!

Sam turned to run back into the house. On the front doorknob, Sam saw a white card with blue writing on it. He plucked it off and began to read it. He ran his fingers over the blue logo and the words G-A-S C-O-M-P-A-N-Y. It was a notice from the gas company. Attached to the notice was a business card with the name "John Johnson, Project Manager" on it. Sam read the note slowly out loud. "Please call me ASAP regarding your gas line." What did that mean and who was John Johnson?

Sam was a kid who asked a lot of questions. He was a bit tall for his age with lots of light brown hair that he wore in a crew cut. He ran to the phone, pushing up his glasses, and began dialing using the speakerphone. "Does this mean they will be digging up the road?" he wondered. "Maybe digging up our yard? Will they be using an excavator and a backhoe?" More than anything, Sam loved watching construction equipment at work. He couldn't resist anything having to do with equipment, digging, or building. His yard was full of tools, materials to build with, and toy construction trucks of all kinds. His closets were full of construction safety gear, such as hard hats, fluorescent vests, earplugs, note pads with drawings of trucks and equipment, and safety glasses. He often sat and watched road or building construction for hours. Sam's interest and determination regarding construction were something distinctly a part of him. Mom said it might be his calling in life—whatever that meant.

A woman answered and said in a friendly, formal voice, "Gas company, how may I direct your call?"

"John Johnson, please," said Sam.

"One minute, please," said the company operator.

"Mr. Johnson's office, may I help you?"

"Could I please speak with John Johnson?" Sam said in his most determined voice.

The voice stifled a chuckle. "He's not here at the moment. Can I take a message?"

"He left us a note," Sam explained. "A note about our gas line and I wondered what Mr. Johnson needs from us. What's he going to do to our gas line? Is he going to dig up our yard? The note said to call right away," Sam blurted out.

"Oh, I see. Well, Mr. Johnson can explain all that to you. I don't know the answers to your questions, but I can tell that you really want to talk to him. I'll leave him a message and tell him to give you a call. What's your name, fella, and your number?"

Sam ran to his closet to grab his construction gear. "C'mon, Mom. Don't you want to see what is making all that noise?" Sam said, putting on his orange safety vest. He stuffed a couple of screwdrivers in the pockets. He wrapped a set of gummy earplugs around his neck. Earlier that day, he had used the Internet to find out how to drive a backhoe. If he got a chance to talk to the backhoe operators, he wanted to be able to sound knowledgeable. He had the printout of the steps folded in his safety vest.

How to Drive a Backhoe:

1. Walk around the backhoe and make sure there are no people, pets, or obstructions in the way. After your safety check, climb up into the driver's seat. Adjust the seat and steering wheel so you can comfortably reach the controls. Insert the key into the ignition and start the backhoe. If the engine hasn't been run in a while, allow it to idle for about 10 minutes.

2. Familiarize yourself with the controls while the engine is warming up. Locate the double brake pedals and the accelerator on the floor. Find the gearshift and the forward and reverse drive lever. To drive a backhoe, you'll also need to locate the levers that lift and curl the front bucket.

3. Turn the seat around so that you're facing the rear of the backhoe. The longer controls operate the boom and the bucket. Make sure the bucket is completely curled in toward the backhoe. Make sure the boom is raised, positioned in the center, and pulled back against the backhoe.

4. Locate the shorter control sticks that raise and lower the stabilizers. Make sure the stabilizers are all the way up before you drive the backhoe.

5. Turn the seat back around. Lift the front loading bucket so it's off the ground a few feet. Make sure it's not so high that it interferes with your visibility. Make sure it's not so low that it touches the ground. Hop off the backhoe and drop the transport-locking pin into place on the front bucket.

6. Climb back into the seat. To drive the backhoe, put your foot on the brake pedals and shift it into gear. Push the forward and reverse lever in the direction you want to go. Release the brakes and push the accelerator pedal to drive the machine.

7. Put the hazard lights on at all times while driving the backhoe.

Sam was chomping at the bit. He wanted to see how many machines were making the noise, what kind of machines they were, and what they were doing. He wanted to get down to the new jobsite as fast as he could.

His neighborhood, the very old town of Sewickley, Pennsylvania, is nestled next to the long and wide Ohio River. Long ago, American Indians walked their farm animals up and down the main street to get to market. A sky blue bridge spans the river and a high mountain rises above the little village in the center of town. The streets are lined with pink magnolia trees in the spring, a big green canopy of shady trees in the summer, and white twinkling lights in the winter.

On Beaver Street, the main street in the village, Sam passed the town's candy store. Usually, his mouth watered when he saw the candy that fizzed or the chocolates in gold foil boxes. But he didn't go inside today like he did most days. He passed right by the small grocery store, the new store going in that was being painted bright green and white, and the coffee shop with the great cakes, buzzing with people.

Sam didn't pay attention to any of the usual sights in the village. For there, across from the bank in the intersection was a large yellow backhoe, pounding away at the road! He only had eyes for that backhoe and the team of workers surrounding the job. Sam pushed his glasses up on his nose and squinted at his mother, pointing to the backhoe. "Mom! A backhoe! And look—the outriggers are out!" He screamed over the noise. Mom smiled and sighed a little because she knew what that meant. She would be standing in the hot sun watching a roaring machine grind through the pavement.

After he had been watching for a while, Sam could feel the grit coming up from the pavement on his skin.

The whole street smelled like soot and oily smoke. Sweat rolled down each of the workers' faces, necks, and backs. Sam was sweating underneath his hard hat and vest too. Sam felt his face were growing red from the heat. He knew he wouldn't be able to stay very long.

ERRRA, ERRRR. ERRRR, RRRRRG. Again, Sam imagined that the machine was saying, "I like to diiiggg and wooorrrkkk." In his imagination, he clearly heard the backhoe saying it loved to work. He squeezed his hands into fists with excitement.

Seizing what time he had and keeping a safe distance, Sam walked toward the worker who had been calling out signals to the crew and the backhoe operator. "Hey!" the worker called to the crew. "Ho!" They yelled toward the backhoe man while giving hand signals to the backhoe man. He was holding his hand up and turning it around in a circle, indicating to the backhoe to keep moving forward. Then, he held his hand up in a fist, meaning to stop. Sam held up his own fist, imitating the man's motion.

"What are you guys doing here? What do those hand signals mean?" Sam asked the man giving the directions.

"Hey, little man. Ain't you all decked out?" The man said, kindly. "We're diggin' up the road so we can get to the gas lines. The gas lines up and down Beaver Street are about 100 years old and need to be replaced."

"Sweet!" said Sam. "How long are you going to be working here? What's your name?"

"You ask a lot of questions, little man." the worker said, laughing. "I'm Scott. I'm in charge on this here job.

This here is Ronny in the backhoe and that's Luis down in the hole."

He pointed down into the 20-feet-by-six-feet trench in what used to be a busy intersection. "This is our first week of the job here and we reckon to be here for three months at least. We're taking out the old gas utility lines and replacing them all up and down Beaver Street with this here new pipe. We are going to be digging trenches all summer, about 30 of these trenches, I reckon. Well, I gotta get back to work."

Sam immediately liked Scott. Scott was tan and strong and had a way of talking that was very warm and friendly. He confidently strode around the jobsite, as if he knew exactly what to do and when. He spoke to Sam as if he was a grown up, and Sam liked that very much.

The enormous gold 410J John Deere backhoe with its large digging claw on the front and front loader scraper blade on the back continued to bang, bang, bang its large conical teeth into the dirt with crushing blows. Each blow dug the trench deeper and deeper. The crew used their shovels to scoop away rocks and broken pavement. The shovels scraped loudly, hurting Sam's ears. The ground shook. Each strike was deafening.

A skid steer loader hauled away the large rock-sized chunks of asphalt and dumped them into a nearby red dump truck with a crash. The vehicles beeped every time they backed up, creating back-up noise to accompany the banging. Cars trying to make their way through the village swerved this way and that. It was difficult for cars to navigate the "roadwork ahead" signs as the flaggers waved red flags.

The huge boom of the backhoe swung the teeth around overhead and back and forth. Sam loved to watch the backhoe operator's hands. Each hand held on to a lever with a knob on top. The hands moved both levers at the same time in different ways. Just then, Ronny the operator jumped out of the cab on the backhoe and swung himself down on the street.

"Hi! You interested in the backhoe?" he asked. "This here's my buddy," he said, patting the side of the backhoe.

"Backhoes are my favorite because they are two machines in one!" Sam exclaimed emphatically, thrilled by the chance to talk to a real backhoe man. Sam had been saying for several years that all he wanted to be when he grew up was a "backhoe man." Ronny laughed out loud, a rousing laugh that shook his very large, muscular body.

"Thatta boy! Well, ain't you the 'Construction Kid'! Yep, hard work is good for the body, the mind, and the soul," Ronny said. "But don't forget to get an education. If you want to run the job someday, you gotta go to school. I gotta go get a drink and some lunch. See you later, Boss," he said to Sam as he threw a huge leg over his shiny silver motorcycle parked nearby.

Sam said, "See ya!" as he watched Ronny wave and zoom off. "Wow!" thought Sam. A real backhoe man. Right in his own neighborhood!

"I wish I could drive that backhoe like Ronny!" Sam shouted, staring at the backhoe. In his mind, the backhoe seemed to shudder and settle down after all that tough work grinding the trench in the road. The backhoe hissed when the motor was turned off. Sam imagined that he saw the backhoe "relax" as it idled to a stop. The noises sounded like words to him. Sam imagined that the backhoe said, "Come and work with me!" He wished more than anything it could be true.

"Hey, you're going to need a hard hat to go with that vest if you're going to be visiting the jobsite, Construction Kid," Scott said, grinning widely, overhearing Ronny giving Sam his new nickname. He tossed Sam a gold hard hat with the words "Fortney Construction" on it. "And maybe one day we will let you sit in the backhoe and drive it—if you're good."

As the crew headed off to lunch, Sam reluctantly waved good-bye. It was early summer, but Sam knew he would have to start the new school year in several weeks. But for now, he was in heaven. From that moment on, Sam was hooked. He felt a surge of energy—a river of energy—running through his entire body. He felt a determination that he did not know how to explain. Sam felt that he was a part of the Fortney Construction crew and he was beyond thrilled.

2

HE CALLED ME "BUDDY"

After that first visit to the jobsite, Sam spent more than a lot of time thinking about construction vehicles. To him, equipment sometimes seemed to act like people. Construction vehicles even looked human to Sam. He often wondered what it would be like if a backhoe, for instance, could think and talk. To Sam, a vehicle's cab looked like a person's head, the lights seemed like eyes, the outriggers or booms seemed like arms, and the pointed forks or cones looked like, and acted like, teeth. All that summer, Sam imagined what the pieces of equipment would say if they could talk to each other. As he walked down the street away from the site, he imagined construction vehicle conversations.

"He called me 'Buddy,'" he thought the backhoe would say, referring to Ronny's nickname for the backhoe. Sam imagined that Buddy would say, "I guess that's my name. I've never had a name before."

In Sam's way of thinking, he imagined that Buddy the backhoe liked his new name very much, and he loved the operator, Ronny, that drove him. He thought that Buddy and Ronny were very in tune with each other as they worked. Ronny knew just how to move the levers with ease so that Buddy didn't jerk his boom or strain his hydraulic system. Sam imagined that Buddy loved how Ronny drove him smoothly down the road, without making Buddy hop or stutter step.

Sam pictured that Buddy also liked how Ronny prepared him for the day and took care of Buddy's mechanical needs. Based on what he knew and had read about construction, he imagined what their daily routine would be like. He imagined that every morning at 6:30 a.m., Ronny did the same thing. He would put on his hard hat, pat the backhoe, and say, "Good morning, Buddy. Let's get to work." Ronny probably used a checklist to get ready for the day, which he (and probably Buddy) knew by heart.

"Buddy, do you have any broken parts? How are your hydraulic hoses? Any cuts or leaks?" Ronny might ask, running his hands over Buddy's hoses. "Your fluid looks a little low. We need to fix that for sure so that you can run smoothly."

Sam bet that Buddy was happy to get a proper amount of hydraulic fluid. He imagined that his favorite part was having his fittings greased; it must feel so good and make it so much easier to move around.

"Let's have a look at your fittings today. They look good except a couple over here. Let me give these a good squirt." Ronny would probably say.

Ronny most likely also carried his grease can along with him during the morning inspection.

"I can take care of greasing these," Sam imagined Ronny would say, pumping his grease gun and squirting lots of lubricating oil on Buddy's "joints." "We're gonna have to get maintenance to give you the spa treatment, though, in a couple of weeks." Ronny laughed at his own joke, as Sam imagined it.

Daily checklist for Backhoe Operation

o   Check for broken or damaged parts, starting with hydraulic hoses for cuts, excessive wear, and leaks.
o   Check that all control levers start in the "off" position.
o   Grease all fittings every eight hours and check the loader's hydraulic-fluid level every day. The backhoe won't operate properly if fluid is low.
o   Plan ahead. Plan your day to maximize productivity at the jobsite:
o   List any tools you need for the backhoe and keep them close at hand.
o   Stake out the area to be excavated and use flags, cones, or paint to mark it.

- o Mark any gas or water lines with flags or tape to avoid hitting them.
- o Never work in areas with inadequate overhead clearances.
- o If the trench is over five feet deep, use shoring equipment, such as sandbags, ladders, or forms, or dig the trench in the shape of a "V" to lessen the possibility of a cave-in.

Sam imagined that Buddy would say, "I love to work! I love to work!" humming loudly, enjoying the tough digging, scooping, and dumping. Buddy loved hard work, Sam was sure of that. Unknown to anyone but himself, Sam imagined conversations that Buddy might have, all that hot summer. While he was doing chores, swimming on the swim team, or while he was working on his "construction jobs" in the backyard, Sam thought about how similar to humans construction vehicles were and what Buddy might think, say, and do. To him, Buddy seemed like a real person.

In Sam's mind, Buddy loved working with Ronny and the Fortney Construction crew. But what Buddy really wanted, as Sam often thought, was to talk to Ronny and the other guys on the crew, to communicate how well they had worked or even how hard it was to work during those brutally hot summer days. He imagined that Buddy tried again and again to talk to Ronny, but that Ronny never seemed to notice. He imagined that if Buddy were a person, he would try to nudge the crew with his bucket, roar extra loudly to get their attention, and even zigzag his tracks down the street to get attention.

Being a person himself, Sam knew Buddy was most likely very disappointed by this. Sam imagined what it would be like if Buddy could move on his own. He thought about how scared Ronny and the crew would be if Buddy raised or lowered his boom by himself. What a surprise that would be to see a backhoe moving on its own! Being the kind backhoe that Buddy was in Sam's mind, Buddy would try to be helpful. Sam imagined that every once in a while, Buddy would help Ronny by moving ever so slightly on his own, leaving Ronny to think that the machine was just well oiled. Buddy would go the extra mile to help out, just like the Fortney Construction crew did for their team.

Sam also pictured in his mind that the other vehicles on the job could also think, talk, and move but did so only to each other. The gigantic excavator on this job was an older model and had little interest in discussing the job or interacting with the crew. The excavator was a big grump. He would ask Buddy, "Why do you want to talk to the crew? What peace and quiet would we have?"

Because Buddy was a hard worker in Sam's way of thinking, Buddy just wouldn't understand this. "If you love working," Buddy would say, "why not talk about it or ask questions to learn more? Wouldn't you like to find out more?"

"I am old, tired, and rusty. I've been on hundreds of jobs. What more can I learn?" the excavator would mumble. This was easy for Sam to imagine, as he had seen several adults act like this before.

Because of the quick-paced action of the skid steer, Sam imagined that it was Buddy's main friend and ally on the job. As far as Sam knew, the skid steer didn't have a nickname. He was just called "skid steer." Sam thought Buddy and the bobcat enjoyed working side-by-side on the job. Sam decided that the skid steer needed a name too, so he decided to call him "Skids."

The next day, while riding his bike to swim team practice, Sam thought back on his recent visit to the jobsite, how Buddy the backhoe seemed to talk, shudder, and sigh. He imagined what Buddy and Skids might have said to each other during that visit while he was watching. Sam imagined that their conversation:

"Whew, what a day! Have you seen how many trips I have made to the dump truck?" asked Skids.

"Yeah—make sure you don't bust a track, Skids!"

"I wish Luis would use that water hose to get rid of some of this dust. My fittings are getting all full of dirt. I get so cranky when I am full of grit."

"You said it, pal. I could use some extra grease right about now. Hey, check out that new man on the crew. He's kind of small, don't you think?"

Buddy gave a short nod of his cab. "He was dressed just like the men in the crew, but he's a lot smaller. "

"I'm guessing this guy is shorter than the bottom of my door!" Buddy continued. "I've seen a lot of people coming and going in the village, but most of them don't take any interest in me. In fact, many of them seem annoyed by my roaring, pounding or scraping bucket. Mothers often cover their little people's ears as they went go by and they make faces at the noises I make."

"Yeah, I see him. But he seems happy and even excited to watch us. Most people do just walk on by..." Skids trailed off.

Sam imagined that Buddy wished he could twist around to get a better look at this little man but that he didn't dare move too much.

"Buddy, he's not a little man. He's a kid!" Skids yelled, wheeling around on his tracks in this make believe conversation. "He just said that backhoes are his favorite machines."

"No way!" Buddy said, excitedly, as he dug through the dirt in the trench. "I gotta get a look at this kid." Buddy yelled out to Skids. Just when Buddy was trying to get Sam's attention, Ronny shut him down and said, "Time for lunch, ol' Buddy."

Sam remembered thinking that it seemed, at that moment, that Buddy sighed as he was turned off. Sam remembered that he had said out loud, "I wish I could drive a backhoe."

"You can! You can! Come work with meeee..." Sam imagined that Buddy had tried to say this as his engines was being turned off. Sam thought Buddy was watching him walk up Beaver Street to a modest, old, red brick house several blocks up the road.

Sam was almost at the pool, but continued to think about what the machines might have said to each other:

"These streets are old but that makes them easy to chew up. The road is like crunching candy toffee," Buddy said. He had seen children with crunchy tan toffee coming out of the village candy shop. "And under the toffee, the rich, dark soil is like a brownie made of dirt. As he dug through the thick brownie dirt with his massive teeth, Buddy would occasionally hit some very old bricks that used to make up the street. "These bricks are nuts in my brownie. Chewing up the road is delicious work for me!"

Sam knew that Buddy was still working all the rest of that hot, summer day while he went to the pool. The daydream continued as he parked his bike at the pool.

"I've been looking for that kid and I am worried he's not coming back soon. I really want to see that kid who dresses like Scott, Ronny, and Luis again. He did say he was coming back, didn't he, Skids?" Buddy asked Skids nervously. Buddy was a bit of a worrier.

Skids was trying to focus on carrying some heavy and long lengths of pipe. "Yes, he's coming back. Don't worry so much," said Skids as he slid another set of pipes off his forks. "You need to take your mind off that kid. How are your hydraulic hoses feeling today?" Skids knew all about hydraulics, but Buddy fancied himself an expert on the topic. Skids knew that if he could just get Buddy to talk about something, it would take his mind off worrying about when Sam was coming back. This is how Sam imagined they would talk to each other.

"Feeling super today, thanks for asking. Sometimes my pistons feel a bit stressed in this hot weather, but not today. I am always concerned about fluid leak, you know. Did I ever tell you how hydraulics work?" Buddy prattled on and on as Skids, the dutiful friend, listened.

"Hydraulic systems use liquids to transmit force between pistons. Imagine that—liquids!" Buddy chuckled.

"Liquids! Ha!" snorted Skids, zooming back over to the dump truck to get more pipes.

Buddy continued. "Pistons are sealed containers that are used to move fluids. They usually use oil because water can cause rust. You see, pistons with oil inside magnify force. This means that when you push a piston, the force of the push can be magnified to move a heavy load with the other piston. A hydraulic system is good because I can lift heavier loads with it."

The dump truck, parked on the side street nearby yawned, uninterested.

"Because the pistons always have to keep moving, a pump powered by my engine pushes the pistons all the time. But, you know, the pistons in a backhoe need to move in different directions in order to move the backhoe in different directions. I can do this because I have other pistons called hydraulic rams. I have a valve that changes the direction the oil is pumped. Isn't that so cool?" Buddy asked to anyone that might be listening.

Skids nodded as he idled nearby.

"This valve is called a spool valve. The valve moves to put oil into different hoses. Sometimes these hoses can break. I sure hate it when that happens...." Sam imagined that Buddy did most of the talking and that he loved talking about his mechanical operations.

"Hey, Sam. Ready to tear it up in the pool today?" Griffin, one of Sam's favorite lifeguards asked.

"Oh, umm, yeah. Tear it up. Right." Sam said, shifting his own mental gears back to focusing on swim team practice.

"Twweeetttt!" Griffin blew the whistle loudly to start the practice. Kids dove into the water, splashing and thrashing down the swim lanes. For the moment, Sam's construction daydreams would have to wait.

Meanwhile, it had been a long, hot day for the Fortney Construction crew. Ronny drove Buddy back to the yard where the crew kept their construction vehicles, supplies, and tools at night. It was next to a very old gray church with an enormous bell tower on top. The yard was a soft green field with a thick canopy of trees overhead that helped keep Buddy and the other vehicles cool and out of the rain.

"Time for your rub down, Buddy. I wish I could have a rub down. Boy, am I tired!" Ronny rubbed most of the grime and sticky coal patch off Buddy's doors, windows, and windshield.

"I sure liked that kid Sam." Ronny called out to Scott who was filling out the report for the day.

"Yeah, he reminds me of me when I was a boy. When I was a kid, I couldn't get enough of organized destruction either!" Scott laughed.

Ronny was so tired, he wished he could "shut down" like a piece of equipment, too. He wondered if machines felt as tired as he did at the end of a long day. Ronny thought that they did. Looking around the yard at the dump truck, the skid steer, Buddy, the excavator, and the generator, it seemed to Ronny in the last light of the day that they all seemed to be asleep.

"Another great day, huh, Buddy?" Ronny said, a bit hoarsely, his voice tired from talking over the noise of the jobsite all day. "You sprawl out here on the grass and settle down for a good long sleep." Ronny said under his breath as he patted Buddy's shovel. "Good night, jobsite." Ronny said, as he strapped on his black, shiny motorcycle helmet.

3

FIRST DAY ON THE CREW

ERRRA, ERRRA, ERRR, clank. ERRRA, ERRA, ERRR, clank. BANG!

Day after day, everyone all over Sewickley could hear the sounds of the construction equipment.

The postman heard it as he walked from house to house.

The teachers at the schools heard the roar and occasional bang as the crew dropped a thick, heavy, iron plate to cover their large trench so that public buses could glide by.

Mom's friend, the writer, could hear it in her attic as she burned through the keys on her computer, writing her next book.

Customers in the hair salon tried to talk over the noise as they discussed hair, nails, and the clever window displays of the latest fashions at the store next door.

People in the village could hear little else as the construction progressed. ERRA, ERRRA, BANG combined with BEEP, BEEP, BEEP.

Sam was excited to see the progress Fortney Construction had made on the huge trench in front of the bank.

"You're late!" Scott exclaimed to Sam, grinning from ear to ear. "You are supposed to be here at 7:00 a.m."

"It's summer and I get to sleep until eight o'clock." Sam grinned back at Scott.

It was now nine a.m. and already very hot, humid, and sticky.

"My main man, how are you today?" Scott said, shaking Sam's tiny hand in his own huge, dirty, and leathery one. Scott's hand looked like a baseball catcher's mitt compared to Sam's hand. "You're lookin' good in your vest, hard hat, and safety glasses. But where are your metal-toed boots, Construction Kid?"

"They don't make them in my size." Sam said, and Scott laughed. "I'm good! What are you working on today?" Sam asked, eagerly.

"Well, today we are on a tight deadline to get this new pipe installed. We have to cap of the other gas lines first. Then we measure and cut the new pipe and fit it into the trench and reconnect the lines. Then we gotta backfill the hole with sand first, then dirt, then coal patch."

"What's coal patch?" Sam yelled over the noise.

"Coal patch is what you put on last to make the top of the hole look like the road again, only not as smooth." Scott said quickly, jogging off toward the crew. "Hey, don't let anyone down in the hole until we get sandbags and a ladder to shore it up. It's over five feet deep now and could cave in. Alex, you grab the sandbags and a ladder, would you?" Scott urged.

"Sure." Alex replied, smiling over at Sam. Sam noticed that Alex, one of the crewmembers, had eyes that crinkled up merrily when he smiled.

"I've got to get some pipe pieces cut. I'll talk with you later, Main Man," Scott yelled over his shoulder. "Hey, watch the length of that pipe!" Scott yelled out to Luis, who was dragging the pipe over to the saw. "Remember, measure twice and cut once!"

Scott was a busy guy, Sam noticed. He noticed that Scott was busy trying to help the crew do the job correctly and safely.

"Measure twice and cut once. Got it," Luis agreed, nodding his head and wiping the sweat off his forehead and then his neck. "Hey, Sam. How's it goin'? I think it's as hot here as it is where I am from in Arizona."

"Why did you come here from Arizona?" Sam asked as Luis worked to set up the saw and the generator.

"It's good work and a good way to show what I can do on the job. I'm hoping to be a foreman sometime soon and this is my chance to show my skills leading the team in the trench."

Sam wondered what it takes to be the foreman of a jobsite. He had watched the Fortney crew and had seen Scott doing his job. It seemed to Sam that being the right kind of foreman was like pulling the right levers at the right time on a machine. Too much of a lever, and the machine would go wacky. Too little, and the machine wouldn't move at all and no work would get done. It was the same with a crew. To be a good leader of a crew, the foreman had to know what levers to pull, how much, and when. Sam thought about these levers and decided to write them down.

Sam's Levers for Leaders

1. Do the job correctly and safely.
2. Solve problems.
3. Work as a team—it's the only way!
4. Keep calm.
5. Be kind.

Sam continued to watch Luis. He and some of the other men on the crew dragged the long yellow pipe over to the saw. The yellow plastic-looking pipe was going to be the new gas line that would funnel gas to all the stores and homes on Beaver Street. Luis showed the old pipe to Sam.

"What on earth is that?" Sam asked, wrinkling up his nose at the thin, brown, shrunken looking piece of pipe the crew had unearthed from the hole.

"That," Luis said, "was that old pipe that doesn't work well anymore. I hear it was first put in the ground in the 1880s. We are going to put in brand new PVC pipe like this, which is stronger, will last longer, and will work better." Luis patted the large yellow pipe. He picked up a short ring of the yellow pipe that looked like a very large cheerio, only yellow. "Here," Luis said. "Feel how heavy this is."

Sam picked up the huge cheerio and almost dropped it on his foot. It was so heavy! "What is PVC pipe?" Sam asked.

"Well, Boss, it stands for polyvinyl chloride, and it's is made from combining plastic and vinyl. The pipes are durable, hard to damage, and long lasting. A PVC pipe does not rust, rot, or wear over time. That's the reason we use it in water systems, underground wiring, and sewer and gas lines," Luis explained to Sam.

Sam looked up at Luis, his mouth hanging open. Sam thought Luis was a very smart and patient man as he continued to watch from a safe distance in the shade.

The crew worked steadily cutting the heavy yellow pipe into pieces and then joining the pieces together with what looked like "elbows" and "knees" to Sam. They were making the long pieces fit into a shape that would go back down in the trench and then hook up to the other lines, completing the replacement of the old lines with newer, stronger lines. To cut the pipes to the correct length, Luis and the crew used a saw that buzzed so loudly that Sam wondered how they "chatted in the outfield" like a baseball team does while they worked.

On Luis's order, the crew hoisted the huge pipe and joint unit up in the air and over to the hole. It took the whole crew to lift it! They strapped it onto the backhoe and the backhoe did the heavy lifting from there. Ronny, at the controls, used the backhoe to lower the pipe unit gently down into the hole. Scott used his hand signals again to tell Ronny when to move forward, lower a lot more or only a bit more, and then to stop. Sam loved those hand signals and used them any chance he got. The night before, he used them when Dad was coming down the driveway with the car from work. He pretended he was Scott, the foreman, directing the car down the driveway and into the garage.

Sam looked around for the backhoe during the pipe fitting work. No backhoe anywhere. "Where was the backhoe?" Sam wondered, a panic coming over him. "Was the backhoe work all done?" He couldn't get anyone's attention to ask.

A man came on the job that Sam didn't know. He was wearing a dress shirt and pants with a white hard hat that read G-A-S C-O-M-P-A-N-Y.

"Hey, maybe that's John Johnson!" Sam yelled out.

"Hey, Johnny!" Scott clapped Mr. Johnson's hand and shook it vigorously like they were old friends. "Come to help us out on this ol' thing?"

"Hey, how's it going? Is the pipe fitting without any leaks? Have you checked for leaks yet?" Mr. Johnson asked.

The two men talked for a while, and then Mr. Johnson walked over to his big white gas company truck. Now was Sam's chance to ask him some questions. Sam ran over to the truck parked safely away from the work site.

"Are you John Johnson?" Sam asked, somewhat out of breath.

"Why, yes, I am." He looked at Sam quizzically. "Who...? Oh, you must be Sam. I got a message that you called. Glad to meet you." He shook Sam's hand.

"What do you keep in this truck?" Sam asked, straining his neck inside the truck to look at the gadgets, papers, files, tools, and other things.

"That's where I keep the tools I need for the job. And, as a matter of fact, I have something just for you right here. My secretary was so tickled when you called. She told everyone in the office. She packed a few things for me to give to you," Mr. Johnson said, grinning.

"Whoa. Thanks!" Sam said. His eyes were as wide as saucers.

Mr. Johnson gave Sam a gas company T-shirt, a Hacky Sack ball with the gas company logo on it, and some stickers. Sam proudly displayed his new prized possessions for the crew to see.

"Lunch!" Scott yelled through his cupped hands to the crew. Many members of the team had brought their lunch from home and were shutting down their machines. Others had bought their lunch at the nearby store. They sat on an old, low brick wall near the jobsite in the shade to eat.

"I'm starving!" Alex, the man with the crinkly eyes, said and started devouring his sandwich.

Off in the distance, they could hear the sounds of the beautiful bells from the nearby church tower. The bells played three songs every day at 12:00, 3:00, 6:00, and 9:00 p.m. Sam loved to listen to the bells when they rang. The bells were loud in their own right and their songs were soothing and calming. The bells felt reassuring to Sam and made him feel that all was right in the world. At night, he would listen to the last bells of the day and hum while he was lying in bed.

Sam was not hungry at all. All he wanted to do was stay there with his team. Without hesitation, Sam marched confidently over to the wall, shimmied his small body in between two of the workers, and sat down as if to have his lunch with them, too.

"Main man, I tell you what," said Scott as he pulled out four sandwiches from his lunch bag. "You bring your lunch another day and you can eat with us. At the end of the job, we can all go out to lunch to celebrate. But, I want to hear good reports on you." To Sam, it was as if Santa Claus had come to town.

4

THE BACKFILLING JOB

S am was so excited about his new crew. He couldn't
wait to talk to Dad about the workers, the machines,
and the jobsite. As Dad drove down the driveway, Sam
ran along the side of the car yelling, "Dad, did you see
my new crew! Did you see them on Beaver Street?"

After dinner, Sam and Dad walked back down to the
jobsite. The crew was working to "backfill" the huge
trench in the road. The backhoe was unloading huge
piles of sand into the hole. Scott was there, hot and tired
after working since 7:00 a.m. that morning.

"Hey, my main man. Want to see how we backfill?"

"Yes! Sam was thrilled to be included in what looked
like a major part of the operation.

"Hello, Dad. You have quite a little worker man here," Scott said, patting Sam on top of his gold Fortney Construction hard hat.

"Yes, Sam's a hard worker all right. He's been obsessed with machines since he was a year old. Did Sam tell you about his first machine, a vacuum cleaner he named 'Tony'?" Everyone in the crew laughed and so did Sam.

"Thanks for the hard hat, by the way," said Dad. "It will come in handy this summer as sun protection." Again, everyone laughed. Dad was good at making people laugh. Sam liked how Dad and the crew seemed to joke around so easily.

Sam could see that Scott and the crew were working hard that evening even though they were hot and sweaty, tired, and dirty from head to toe. They were strong men and knew exactly what to do to get the job done right. Sam admired this very much. He wanted to be strong and know what to do next at the jobsite himself. More than anything, he wanted to be able to drive the backhoe.

Sam watched the backfilling operation. It was exciting because it involved filling the hole first with sand, then dirt and gravel, and then smoothing coal patch on top. Filling a huge trench was a major job for four machines: the dump truck, the backhoe, the mini packer, and the bobcat. First, the dump truck went to the "yard" or the area where mounds of sand, dirt, and coal patch were stored. Then, the dump truck came back to the jobsite to be unloaded. Unloading the dump truck required lots of hand signals, yelling out of orders, and coordination among the crew. The crew's tight coordination made the job look effortless, Sam thought.

Next, the backhoe scooped up huge mounds of sand to fill the trench, dump the sand in the trench, and then go back for more. While it was scooping, Sam imagined what the backhoe might be saying. The backhoe engine roared and the boom clanked, but it sounded like words to Sam.

"I like to dig. I like to woooorrrkkk. Come and wooorrrkk with me!"

Sam thought to himself. "This is so cool. I feel like I can actually hear the backhoe telling me what its thinking."

Alex and Luis jumped in the trench and smoothed out the sand to cover all the pipes evenly. They even let Sam hold one of the shovels off to the side of the trench! With Ronny in the backhoe, the rest of the crew repeated the backfill process with dirt, and then came the gooey, smelly coal patch. Coal patch is a combination of sticky tar and gravel that oozes out of the backhoe bucket. Sam thought it looked a lot like the molasses he had seen Mom use to make gingerbread cookies. Then, the crew quickly spread the coal patch over the trench.

"Doesn't that smell good?" Sam said to Luis, pointing to the coal patch.

"Wonderful," said Luis, holding his nose against the strong stench.

"Can I help spread the coal patch?" Sam said, looking longingly to Ronny and then to Scott.

"Sure, Boss," said Ronny. "Help show these guys how to do it right. See, like this." Ronny showed Sam how to smooth the sticky coal patch with the shovel in the right direction. Sam was in heaven, shoveling like a real worker! His legs had splotches of black, tar-like coal patch on them, but he didn't care.

That evening, at least 100 cars must have driven by, some slowly minding the flaggers and some driving a bit too fast, hurrying to get to where they were going. Many people drove by and waved at Sam. He knew some of the people and he would shout out and wave back to them. Other people he didn't know, but he waved anyway. It seemed that many people loved construction.

One person in the neighborhood clearly did not like construction. Her name was Mildred Finklebottom and she was 82 years old. Old Mrs. Finklebottom was a bony, bent over woman with a shrill voice that was hard on the ears. She did not like anything that disrupted the routine of her quiet life in Sewickley. She was crotchety and complained to Mr. O'Hara, the town manager, about everything. She had already been in his office complaining about the Fortney Construction work, claiming the machines rumbling down the road were shaking the antique windows in her house and keeping her up at night.

Mrs. Finklebottom was out walking her equally old looking, tiny wirehaired dog, Tootsie. Despite the heat, she was wearing a long, green plaid jacket. It seemed to Sam that they both walked as if their hinges had twinges and needed some oil. They walked up to Scott.

"Uh oh, here comes trouble," said one of the crew-members under his breath.

"Is there any chance you boys could stop that racket after dinner time? That's when I watch my programs and I can't hear over all your noise," she shrieked.

The crew was taken aback by her unfriendly tone and screeching voice.

"Well, hey there. Are you Mrs. Finklebottom? I'm Scott and I'm the foreman on this here job." Scott stuck out his hand so that she could shake it, but she ignored it.

"Your noise exceeds the limits of the Occupational Safety and Health Administration, OSHA, you know. I want something done about that." She pointed her bony finger at Scott.

Scott opened his mouth to respond, but she left before he could say a word.

"Hmmphf," she muttered, as she tugged Tootsie away on his leash down the sidewalk, his little neck straining against her pulls.

"Her voice exceeds OSHA limits," joked Chuck.

Sam thought that was a good one. Scott just shrugged his shoulders and kept on working.

Chuck was one of the younger guys on the crew and had the job of running the packer on the coal patch to pack it down before the bobcat came to pack it down some more and smooth it out so that it would look like the road.

An older man with white hair on the crew who had the words "Father Time" on the back of his vest said to

Sam, "Packing is a young man's job." Sam could see that holding the packer straight while it went up and down like a jackhammer, with the same amount of noise, was hard to do. He wondered how Chuck could hold the packer straight without hitting his foot.

"I want to rent a packer to use on my birthday!"

Father Time and Chuck laughed.

After the packing was complete, the skid steer came out to run back and forth over the coal patch. The tracks of the skid steer pressed the coal patch down to a very flat surface matching the height of the road. It was a perfect black patch to cover the trench, almost as if the enormous trench had never been there just hours before.

By the time the trench was covered, it was getting dark out. The bells at the church started playing their songs for 9:00 p.m. "Bell time!" Sam exclaimed. The cicadas were screeching out their summer song, sounding like miniature versions of the saws used on the jobsite to cut the pipes.

Sam said good-bye to the crew and started walking home. Ronny yelled over his shoulder, "Better use some baby oil or mayonnaise to get that coal patch off your legs, or your mom will take your skin off cleaning you!" Sam nodded, laughing.

It had been one of the best days of his life. Sam couldn't stop thinking and talking about Scott, Ronny, Luis, Alex, Chuck, Father Time, and the other members of the crew. He felt a determination inside. He wanted to learn everything he could about construction. Sam felt it like a gravitational pull. He knew he wanted to grow up to be a backhoe man or maybe a boss on a team like Fortney Construction.

At bedtime, Sam closed his eyes and ended that special day saying, "Thank goodness for Fortney Construction, my new crew." He lay still as he looked at the large moon shining brightly into his bedroom. It seemed as bright as a flashlight shining down on him. The gentle rustling of the trees lulled him into a half sleep. He imagined that instead of the moon shining in his room, it was the backhoe shining its light into his room. Sam's mind drifted as he fell off to sleep.

He began to dream. In his dream, he saw that the trees rustling was actually Buddy making noise. He dreamt that at the back of the house, Buddy crept along, so as not to be seen. Buddy was trying to figure out which room was Sam's. The huge backhoe stood on the tip of his tracks and steadied himself against the house with his boom and bucket. His boom was screeching and his tracks were rattling. In the dream, Buddy was trying to keep the noise at a low level so that he could sound like a construction vehicle working late in the night.

At the first window, Buddy peered into a small room with an odd, small, white shiny chair with some water in it. "No, not that one," Buddy whispered in the dream. "That looks like the Johnny on the Spot porta-potties on the jobsite."

Then, he came to the next window in the dream. "I can't quite reach up high enough to see." Buddy stretched with all his might. "Just a little higher and I can just see over the second floor window ledge." He stretched again and then he saw him. There was Sam, tucked in his bed, asleep under his quilt. The quilt was covered with brightly colored backhoes, excavators, and bobcats.

"Awesome room! Look at all the vehicles. He really does love construction!" Buddy stared at the construction cones on the walls, the large toy crane, and the red and white cement mixer at the foot of Sam's bed. Sam, half-asleep and still dreaming, sat up abruptly in bed.

"Huh?" Sam figured he was dreaming, but he could have sworn he heard rustling outside his window. He slumped back down in his bed.

Sam's dream continued. Buddy ducked under the window just in time. Sam flopped back down on his back and began snoring loudly.

"Maybe he's dreaming about me and about the work we could do together," Buddy said in the dream. "I bet he's dreaming of being a backhoe man on a big job, and he and I are digging huge trenches!"

And Sam was.

5

THE GOLDEN RULES OF
TRENCHING

S am woke up the next morning after tossing and
turning in his covers for a few minutes. He could
have sworn he saw or heard something at his window
the night before. Thoughts were running through his
head in rapid fire. What was it? Some kind of monster?
No, not a monster, but whatever it was, it sounded big.

"That was some weird dream," he thought to himself. Then he sprang out of bed. He flew to the door of his
room, excited to get his gear on and head down the street
to join his crew. Suddenly, his feet became heavy, as if
his shoes were full of concrete. He stopped in his tracks.

Today was the first day of nature camp! He thought to himself, hands on his hips. He knew that nature camp was running all week. He liked the idea of camp, but now he wouldn't be able to spend time on the jobsite!

All morning during nature camp, Sam thought about the mysterious dream of the visitor at his bedroom window. While he was absentmindedly painting the birdhouse he had made in camp that morning, he tried to remember exactly what he saw. He painted his thumb a couple of times before realizing he wasn't concentrating on painting the birdhouse at all. Was it a dream about a backhoe? He just couldn't remember clearly. All he could think about was getting back to the jobsite.

"Mom, if I help you plant flowers after camp today, can I go and see Fortney Construction?" Sam looked hopefully at his mom.

"Will you plant and clean up afterwards? Sweep the dirt away *and* carry the tools back to the garage?" Mom asked.

"It's a deal!" Sam nodded. He loved working with the tools in the garden. He used the wheelbarrow as a dump truck and the shovel as a backhoe. Gardening construction, Sam thought. "Cool. I will make the trenches for you to put the plants in, too."

After the gardening construction was finished, Sam went to the jobsite and listened from a safe distance on the sidewalk. Scott and his crew were struggling with fitting the new pipe configuration into the trench, capping the old gas lines, and hooking the new pipes to the gas lines. All this work was called a "tie-in."

"These tie-ins are going to be tough on this job given all the other lines down here. We are going to have a job on our hands this summer, guys. We need to be sure not to cut any water or sewer lines," Scott reminded the crew, yelling over the hum of the generator that provided power for the tools.

Luis was down in the trench, wrestling with the pipes and tools. "This is the wrong cutting tool for this pipe! This is not going to work."

"Hey, who can get Luis the right tool for this? Alex, can you find it? Luis, you stay in the trench. You are the best trench man we have for that job," Scott said, laying his foreman's clipboard down on the top of the truck.

"I know. That's because I am the only one down here all the time!" Luis joked.

Tools and cones were strewn all over the rim of the trench. The generator hummed loudly. The skid steer and the dump truck were nowhere in sight. The backhoe was parked nearby, but it was turned off because it was not part of the tie-in work. Sam walked over to the backhoe and touched the tracks. He put one foot on the bottom stair of the ladder going up the vehicle's side. Sam stood looking at the backhoe in amazement like it was a rocket ship that had just returned from Mars. He was trying to imagine what it might be thinking, if it could think.

He went back to the sidewalk near the action in the trench.

"Sam, you know you need to stay in school if you want to operate a backhoe, don't you?" Scott asked. "You know, working on a construction team is hard, dirty work and plus, you have to work with fellas like these." He said, rolling his eyes, joking, and pointing to Luis, Ronny, Father Time, and Alex, smiling.

"I just want to be a backhoe man and operate in a crew like you guys," Sam said, pointing back at Buddy.

"Well, you have to be smart to run a backhoe and to put these tie-ins just right. You also need to know how to work a computer and run the math for equipment maintenance too. It's tougher than you think. It's not just about jumping down in a hole."

"That's right," said Ronny. "So how did you make it, Scott?"

All the crew belly laughed.

Scott waved him off in a friendly, joking way. Fortney Construction had finally begun the last phase of work for the day: backfilling. Sam knew that backfilling involved a roaring, clanking backhoe.

Scott happily supervised the scooping and dumping of load after load of massive amounts of crystalline sand piled by the side of the trench. He watched as Sam pointed to the trench, talking with Luis. He was impressed that Sam was not afraid to ask questions about the work, the machines, and the tools. He even asked the crew members how they were doing that day. Not only that, but Sam wasn't afraid to pick up a shovel himself and scoop dirt away from the hole. Scott admired Sam's initiative and his smart questions.

"Beats sitting in front of video games all day," Scott thought to himself.

Sam continued to watch the crew and Buddy and thought that he and the machine had a lot of things in common. Sam imagined that Buddy would ask lots of questions just like Sam, if he could. For example, Sam bet that Buddy would want to know why backhoes were Sam's favorite machines. Sam thought another thing they had in common was liking levers, digging, being on a construction site and the Fortney crew.

"How's it going now?" Sam asked, as he looked around at the traffic cones blocking the street and the "Road Closed" signs.

"Slower than a three-legged cow in quicksand!" Luis replied, smiling, as he took off his hard hat and wiped a towel over his sweat-soaked hair. Luis had a way of being calm and cool, even when it was blistering hot out and the job was taking longer than it should.

Sam burst out in laughter. Scott chuckled and nodded his head.

"My main man, Sam. The Construction Kid. Checkin' on our progress? Luis, how's it goin'?" Scott asked.

"Just ready now to boom it down," replied Luis.

"We need all the help we can get. Hey, did you guys find that packer?" Scott called out to Alex and Father Time.

Sam listened quietly but impatiently to Scott. He couldn't wait to see the booming down of the dirt. Booming it down, or packing with the backhoe bucket, would be one of Buddy's best tricks, Sam thought. Ronny moved Buddy's left and then right levers to start to smooth the sand down with the top side of Buddy's bucket. Ronny loved to show off how gently he could smooth out the sand without bumping any of the workers or lines below. It took quite a bit of finesse and skill between Ronny and Buddy to smooth like this. Ronny knew how to do it just right.

Buddy heard Sam yell out with delight. "Wow, the backhoe can work like a grader too. It smoothes the sand down just like a grader." Ronny was pleased and proud that Sam liked his smoothing abilities.

Next, Alex, the man with the crinkly eyes, drove the enormous dump truck to the site, this time full of rocks.

"Here come your rocks, Ronny," Father Time called to Ronny. "I'm ready to dump."

Ronny relied on the red dump truck to dump the loads in just the right spot so that Buddy could easily scoop them.

Out sprayed the rocks onto the pavement with a roar like a massive wave pouring over the jobsite. Sam loved the rock phase of backfilling because the rocks were like crunchy and crumbly food for the backhoe's "teeth." Scraping and scooping up the rocks didn't hurt Buddy's teeth or bucket one bit, Sam noticed. Buddy looked super strong as he moved back and forth with very little jerking or straining. Sam loved the sheer power of the machine.

"I love to worrrkk. Being a backhoe is awesome!" Sam imagined Buddy would shout out if he could talk.

"The new yellow gas lines will be safe and sound now," Scott said proudly. Sam knew the new yellow gas lines would be protected and cozy in their new back-filled home underground.

"Time to buff it up!" yelled Scott, as the crew each grabbed a broom or a shovel.

"Can I help buff? I've done it before," Sam said.

"Buffing" meant cleaning in construction talk.

"Sure. Grab you a broom and get to buffing." Scott said, handing Sam a broom. Sam got to work.

"Hey—you are a better buffer than some of the guys!"

All the guys on the crew either nodded their heads or laughed at Scott.

Sam liked to laugh with the crew. He loved asking them questions about their work and storing their answers in his memory.

"Scott, what are the main rules about digging a trench?" Sam asked.

"Well, my main man. It's like this. There are some key rules. Let's call them 'The Golden Rules' of trenching."

Scott was becoming very fond of Sam. He couldn't believe that Sam was so interested in construction. Occasionally, a few other kids would stop and look at the trench or the backhoe, but they didn't stay long. Talking to Sam made Scott's day go by just a little faster and made it a little more fun. It was a joy to see a kid take so much interest in his job.

"He's bound to go into a design or building related job someday," thought Scott.

"When I am finished with you, Sam, you will know the secrets of trenching and be a pro operator." These words were a sweeter sound to Sam than all the bells in the church tower.

Scott continued. "First, when you begin diggin' with your backhoe, starting at one end of the trench with the machine positioned so you can move backward as you dig your hole. Second, lower the front stabilizers, then the rear stabilizers. Next, you want to dig making square sides and flat bottoms. You have to cut the dirt just so or the edges might cause a cave-in. Of course, you have to use top equipment like one here."

Sam imagined that Buddy puffed up with pride at hearing this.

"That's so cool!" marveled Sam.

"Ronny here has to dig within the marks we've laid out so that we don't hit anything we don't want to hit down there. Then, we put these here steel plates on the sides to prevent cave-ins."

It was almost dinnertime. The backfilling process was in full swing. Sam desperately tried to think of how he could spend more time at the jobsite without going home for dinner. Sam noticed that Ronny and the backhoe were going to and from the yard to get the sand, gravel, and dirt. More than anything in the whole world, Sam wanted a chance to ride in that backhoe. He wanted so much to ask Scott if he could ride along to the yard and back with Ronny.

"Scott, do you think I could get a ride in that backhoe? Could I ride to the yard and back with Ronny?"

"Yep, I think we can do that," said Scott.

Scott yelled up to Ronny in the cab. "The Construction Kid Sam here would like a couple of rides to the yard and back. Let him drive and see how he does," Scott joked.

"Drive!" Sam exclaimed. His face lit up like Fourth of July fireworks. "Me, actually *drive* the backhoe?"

Sam couldn't believe what he was hearing. He felt like his own engine was revving up to full power at this news.

"Sure, hop in. At least it's air conditioned in here and you won't fry outside in the heat!" Ronny was glad to have some company. He enjoyed Sam's direct questions and how Sam laughed at things when the other guys did, even if he didn't quite understand what they were laughing about.

As Sam grabbed the handrail leading up to the cab, a jolt of energy raced up his arm and through his body. He climbed the stairs up to the cab and instantly felt at home. The cab was very enticing and he wanted to soak up every detail of it. It smelled like a combination of dirt, leather, and grease.

Ronny sat Sam at the front of the driver's seat. Ronny sat at the rear of the seat. Sam's legs were too short to reach the gas and brake pedals. Ronny explained the steering, the right and left levers and how they worked. Some of the levers moved the boom forward and backward. Others made the bucket move up and down. The seat could swivel around so that it could face the controls at the back of the backhoe. Sam was trying to listen to Ronny and memorize every word. As they were working, he imagined he was hearing the back-hoe speaking. It started as a rumble or a roar. Then, the rumble and roar morphed into words that sounded like the backhoe was saying his name.

It sounded like, "Sam. Sam, can you hear me?"

"Ronny, do you ever think sometimes that Buddy can talk?" Sam asked Ronny.

"Talk?" Ronny asked in surprise. "Well, I reckon he does talk in his own way now, don't he?"

Sam wasn't sure if he was dreaming or imagining, but in his mind, the backhoe was saying, "Sam, I know you love machines and construction. I want to help you be the builder you can't wait to be!"

Ronny broke into Sam's daydream. "Now, let's go get that gravel. You got the wheel. Ready to help me, Sam?"

Sam had never been more ready for anything in his whole life.

6

EVENING RIDES

All that evening, Sam and Buddy rode back and forth from the jobsite to the yard getting rock, dirt, and finally coal patch to backfill the trench. Donnie and Dave, the flaggers at each end of the jobsite, redirected cars off Beaver Street and onto the side streets. Beaver Street usually had heavy traffic just about any time of day, so it was quite peaceful in the evenings without all the traffic.

Ronny let Sam drive the backhoe up and down the street on his lap sitting on the front tip of the driver's seat. He even let Sam stretch to press the gas while he was steering the wheel! Sam had driven his own electric gator around the yard and on the sidewalks of Sewickley many times when he was younger. It had a gas pedal, but it was nothing like driving Buddy. Buddy's steering wheel felt almost as big around as a Hula-Hoop to Sam.

At first, Sam pressed the gas too far and then too little, causing Buddy to actually hop up and down on the street. Ronny and Sam laughed hysterically at this.

"Sam, you are driving crazy and giving me the hiccups!" Sam imagined Buddy saying.

"Sorry, I've never driven before." Sam laughed to Ronny and to Buddy.

"It's okay. You drive better than Father Time and Chuck already," said Ronny with a smirk.

Up to the yard and back to the jobsite they went. Each time they passed someone he knew on the sidewalk, Sam waved and smiled ear to ear. Two of the passersby were Lauren and her older sister Lindsey. Lauren lived behind Sam and came over to his yard almost every day. She was a year older than Sam was; she was a sporty girl with short, straight blond hair. Able to sink baskets since she was three, Lauren was very athletic. She was super fun and one of his best friends. What Sam liked about her was how she liked working in his "equipment rental shop" in the backyard. She carried the clipboard and kept track of what was "rented" to other kids in the neighborhood. Lauren pointed at the backhoe as she walked, staring in disbelief as she realized Sam was in the driver's seat, hands on the steering wheel, driving the backhoe.

"Yeah, it's me—driving a real backhoe down the street!" Sam exclaimed proudly as they cruised down the street riding high in the air on a roaring machine. It was one of his proudest moments. To Sam, nothing could top driving a backhoe with a genuine, real construction crew on an actual construction site. He hoped that they could avoid seeing old Mrs. Finklebottom. He didn't want her to see him and possibly complain to Mr. O'Hara about him driving the backhoe down the street. Since it was evening, she was probably watching old people shows, like *Jeopardy*.

"You're about as good a worker as anyone here, Construction Kid," Scott said when they pulled the backhoe to a stop. Sam did feel like a real construction worker and part of the crew. Sam thanked Ronny for the rides and as he reluctantly stepped down out of the cab and started back for home.

"Yep, we'll see ya tomorrow, Boss. It's just about quittin' time for us, too. Thanks for all the help and have a good night." Ronny waved.

"Hey, main man. I got a couple of traffic cones here with cracks on 'em. Know anyone who might want 'em?" Scott said, winking at Sam.

"Wow, you mean to keep? Yes, I love construction cones! I can use these in my construction rental business. It's a backyard type of operation," Sam explained. "Thanks! I'm gonna set them up in my backyard!" Sam shouted after Scott who was packing up.

Scott waved. "See ya tomorrow, main man!"

Sam almost flew home on wings. He had some real traffic cones and he had gotten to drive a real backhoe! His mind was racing as he thought about the drive—roaring what seemed like a mile high down the road. He wondered what his friend Lauren would say to him the next time she came to their backyard equipment rental shop. He couldn't wait to tell her all about it.

Back at home, Sam read his favorite book, *Construction Town*, and then turned out the lights. The church bells chimed loudly as they played their beautiful nightly songs. As he was falling asleep, he could still here the rumbling and roaring of the giant backhoe ringing in his ears. It was as if he could still hear Buddy rumbling down the street. He strained his ears to see if he could hear Buddy's tracks and engine roaring down the street. He thought he heard a faint engine roar, and it was getting louder.

Sam slowly got out of bed and crept to his window. His window had a bench seat and shutters covering the windows on the inside. Sam looked out in the darkness of the side yard of his house. Trees swung back and forth, their leaves quietly rustling in the wind. The cicadas sang their summer song. His head was heavy. His whole body was tired and he felt worn out. He laid down on the window bench, his head resting uncomfortably in the bed of a toy dump truck.

Sam was so tired that he fell asleep on the window seat. He started to dream.

As he dreamed, out in the darkness, Sam saw a large shadow looming toward the house. He was frightened a bit at first in the dream, but then he was relieved to see his new friend, Buddy, gently eking his way toward Sam's window.

"It's you. Hey, were you here last night? I had a weird feeling that something big was at my window," Sam said in the dream.

"Hi. Glad to see you, too," Buddy quipped. "That was no dream. It was me! I followed you to your house last night. Cool room, by the way."

"Thanks. Won't you get into trouble for being out of the yard at night?" Sam asked.

"Yeah, plenty, if someone sees me. They might think you took me home, along with those cones I see back there," Buddy joked, creaking a little too loudly.

"Shhh, my mom might hear you."

"Right. So, what do you want to talk about tonight?" Buddy asked in a hushed voice.

"What about the other vehicles—can they talk, too?" Sam asked in the dream.

"Oh yeah. Skids the skid steer is my best friend on the crew. He and I help each other on the job. You have to meet him. The dump truck can talk, but he doesn't say too much. He's kind of a sleepy, slowpoke. The big excavator is just a big grump. I don't talk to him too much."

"For real?" Sam asked.

"Well, only you can hear me so far, but if you can hear me, I bet you can talk to the other vehicles too."

"Sweet! I'm going to talk to them tomorrow." Sam, still in a deep sleep, slowly slid down the window ledge and onto his bedroom floor with a thud. The dump truck he had been using as a pillow crashed to the floor. Sam was still sound asleep and his dream continued.

"What else do you want to know?" Buddy asked. "I am an expert on hydraulics and trenching, ya know."

"Yes, I want to know all about your hydraulics. Tell me about that."

In this spectacular dream, Sam and Buddy talked about hydraulic pistons and pressure. They talked about hydraulic hammers, valves, and pumps.

"There's this thing called the Internet. Have you heard of it?" Sam asked.

"No, is it something you use to haul gravel and dirt?" Buddy asked.

"No, it's even more amazing than that. It's a thing you use on the computer to find out stuff. You would have to meet me on the other side of the house, by the kitchen window, around nine at night. I can show you lots of cool videos of construction sites. I have them saved on the computer downstairs. I have even put videos of you on the Internet, Buddy."

"Hey, that sounds like fun. Maybe I can bring Skids along, too."

"Well, I think that might make a bit too much noise outside the kitchen window," replied Sam.

Buddy thought about that for a second and then said, "Good thinking. Hey, I wanted to tell you to come visit us in the yard after the workday is done. You can sit in me and work the levers and stuff. I'll unlock my doors so you can get in. You just climb up my ladder steps and hop in and then—"

"Sam, what's that noise? Who are you talking to?" Mom asked, appearing at the door in her nightgown.

Tossing a blanket over him as he lay on the floor, Mom sighed. "Well, I guess he was just talking in his sleep again. Maybe overtired," Mom thought as she closed Sam's bedroom door a smidge.

Sam lay there, dreaming about the adventures he would like to have with Buddy in the days ahead.

7

TOUGH DAY

Weeks passed. Over the course of those hot weeks that summer, the Fortney Construction crew dug trenches, buried pipe, hooked up new yellow gas pipes, and backfilled the trenches all along several miles of Beaver Street and many side streets. The crew's equipment buzzed, grinded, scraped, clanked, roared, banged, and beeped all day every day and late into the evenings, just as they had earlier in the summer. And Sam was there many of the days, watching in his hard hat, getting to know the crew and their operation, as he followed them from street to street, jobsite to jobsite, throughout the neighborhood.

One of his favorite adventures was to visit Buddy in the evenings after the work was done, just like in his dream. Sometimes in the evenings, Sam would visit Buddy, Skids, and the other equipment in the yard by the church. Buddy always unlocked his doors when he saw Sam coming for a visit so that he could climb up in the cab. (Or, at least that's what Sam thought; Buddy's doors were always unlocked anyway.) During these visits, Sam loved to turn Buddy's lights on and off. He was amazed some of the lights actually came on without starting up Buddy's engine. He pretended to drive Buddy, moving the steering wheel back and forth and touching the levers. He was careful not to break anything but he couldn't resist trying to figure out what the dials and buttons did. This was the real thing and, for Sam, no computer or video could come close to being as fun as being inside Buddy's cab.

Sometimes during the evenings, Sam was not able to go to the yard. On these nights, he imagined that Buddy would come to the kitchen window to see what construction videos Sam had picked out for them to watch on the Internet. Sam's favorite videos were on the Fortney Construction website. Sam watched these videos almost every day that summer. The founder of the company talked about the purpose of the company and what they expected of every worker. Sam learned a lot about safety, efficiency, hazards, and other complicated construction terms that sounded cool. What Sam learned most from the videos was about how Fortney Construction was special because the employees worked as a team and had integrity. According to the company owner, the way that Fortney Construction teams worked together and treated its customers made all the difference in the world to the company's success. Sam hoped he could meet the owner of Fortney Construction one day or maybe even own his own construction company.

Safety Video

A narrator says,"*Efficiency is the key to lowering cost per ton. Continuous training of operators is important. Operators must understand vehicles' systems and controls to ensure general safety. That includes operating procedures for walk-around inspections, getting started, digging and loading, and shutdown procedures. Read the manual thoroughly for safe operating practices. When conducting your walk-around inspection, look at excess wear on the bucket. Be sure covers and guards are in their proper places. Remove trash, mud, or rocks from the stairs and tracks. Make sure to use the grab irons that provide three-point support at all times.*"

Sam wondered what Buddy would say about efficiency, walk-around inspections, and shutdown procedures. He wondered what Buddy would say about his list of "Levers for Leaders." It was fun for Sam to imagine what Buddy would say about the videos he took of Buddy working at the jobsite.

"Did you see how I dug the lines on that trench so cleanly? And I work fast, don't I, Sam?" he imagined Buddy saying.

"Yeah, you're pretty awesome," Sam would reply.

"And I look good, too. Hardly any rust or dents on me."

"Well, hardly any rust on me, either." Sam smiled through the open window, as if Buddy was standing there like a neighborhood friend.

"And, I am waaayyy more efficient than other vehicles, don't you think?" Buddy might ask.

"Oh sure. No other vehicle can do all the jobs as quickly and as well as you do, Buddy," Sam agreed.

As the summer went on, almost every day after chores, Sam was on the jobsite to watch, ask questions, and help where he could. He painted lines for digging on the street with chalk paint that Ronny gave him. He helped hold the measuring tape. He shoveled dirt and coal patch off the road and into trenches. He brought the team ice when they ran out. He even brought them ice cream on a couple of hot days when he thought they needed a treat.

One time, Sam brought ice cream bars right before lunchtime. He offered one to Ronny. Ronny said, "Aww, that's really nice, but I think I should save it for later, after lunch." Then Ronny thought for a second and said, "Okay, that's later enough." He opened the ice cream and ate the whole thing in two bites with his enormous mouth. Sam laughed hysterically.

One day in particular, the rain poured down without stopping. Thunderstorms and lightning made it impossible for the crew to work. It was raining straight down and sideways. The heavy rain made little rivers on either side of Beaver Street. The clouds were heavy and dark. The light outside was very dim, making it seem like it was late evening instead of first morning light.

Sam ran around the house that morning full of energy. He wondered how the crew was going to be able to work in the bad weather. As he ran around full of anxious concern, he began to get a terrible stomachache. He bent over in pain in front of his mother.

"Mom, I feel a terrible pain in my stomach, but I want to visit the jobsite now."

Mom said, "Let me see. Where does it hurt?" She poked her finger into Sam's stomach, just a bit. At that moment, Sam's body exploded. He loudly burped and tooted from his back end at the same exact time. Mom and Sam howled with laughter for quite a long time at the unexpected "blasts" that came from Sam's body. He felt much better after that!

"Now I'm ready to go to the new jobsite on Academy Street!" Sam proclaimed.

The terrible weather was not a great way to start the huge jobsite at the big intersection of Academy and Beaver. Traffic was always heavy there—so heavy that the intersection actually had a traffic light. The rain was making the traffic even worse.

"Look how the traffic is piling up!" he said, pulling the curtains back from the window. He saw a large, white tent out in the road.

"What on earth?" Sam thought to himself.

Running down the street towards the tent in his raincoat, Sam yelled, "Hi Ronny! Hi Scott!" If the construction site noise hadn't already awakened the neighbors, Sam's yelling must have.

"Main man, how you doin' today?" Scott called back.

"Good. What's that tent for?" Sam yelled, leaning across the white porch railing.

"We're startin' a circus out here," Scott joked, his phone in one hand and a shovel in the other. "Naw, just jokin'. It's how we stay dry and keep the jobsite dry in a storm like this. It's supposed to rain for three days. We got a deadline to meet to get this job done, so we have to keep workin.'" Scott shook his head, hopped in his blue truck, and sped away. It seemed to Sam that Scott was always hustling from one task to the next.

Sam knew he was not going to be happy unless his nose was under that tent and looking in that trench. He approached the big white tent from a safe distance. The men were huddled around the trench under the tent, trying to keep dry and figure out what to do next on the job. Sam was met with a rousing good morning and beaming smiles all around. "Hey, it's the Construction Kid!" or "Good morning, Boss!" came from each of the eight Fortney Construction crew working that day. It was as if Sam being there helped the crew feel just a little better about being soaking wet, hot, and frustrated with the job at hand that morning.

"Where are my doughnuts, Boss?" Luis asked with a chuckle. Sam thought that was hilarious.

"How about some baloney sandwiches later, since you didn't bring the doughnuts?" Luis asked and the other guys all waited for Sam's response.

"I could bring that. What's baloney?" Sam asked, looking up at the crew.

Everyone laughed heartily. Luis rubbed Sam's hooded head with his glove. Working together under that tent in the bad weather had created a jovial, party atmosphere in which Fortney Construction made the best of a tough day.

Luis jumped down in the trench. It was clear from the dirt on his protective suit that he had already been down in the trench that day.

"You're dirty already, Luis," Sam observed.

"Getting dirty makes you feel like you are working hard," Luis replied, jabbing a shovel into the dirt.

Buddy the backhoe was finishing up the digging part of the job. He gave some extra snorts and beeps as his own "good morning" to Sam, Sam imagined. Sam waved to Ronny and then held up both thumbs in the "thumbs up" sign.

Scott had just arrived with a new device in his truck.

Scott leaned down over the hole. "You still shorin' that up? What help do you need?" he asked Luis.

"Workin' on it," Luis shot back, working quickly.

To Sam, Luis seemed to be the one that was always in the trench with the tools, unhooking pipes or trying to configure the new yellow pipes and wires in the hole. It seemed like Luis knew exactly what to do and could do it the fastest. Besides, he fit in the hole the best and was super strong at digging, lifting, and getting in and out of the hole.

Cars whizzed by the jobsite. Dave and Diana, the flaggers, directed traffic to make sure everyone safely navigated around the busy intersection. An old sea foam green car drove by slowly with its window rolled down. The car stopped right in front of the jobsite. It was Mrs. Finklebottom. Sam's heart sank. He remembered her complaints and threats from the last time she came by the jobsite. Her puffy white hairdo was covered with a yellow plastic rain bonnet tied underneath her droopy chin. She leaned over so that she could shout out the window.

"When are you going to finish this mess?" she asked anyone and no one in particular. Her voice sounded very raspy and old but her face looked even older. She did not seem happy.

"Hello there, ma'am," said Scott. "We are doing our best to finish this last site here, ma'am."

"You are tying up traffic here. Your racket is too loud. It shakes my windows. If my windows break, you will hear from me! Do you hear? Hmmpff!" she said as she sped off.

Everyone breathed a collective sigh of relief.

"She was the one tying up traffic with her complaining," thought Sam.

Then it happened. Blam! BLAM! BLAM!

"What the—" Scott started to say.

Ronny looked at the control panel.

"Oh, no." The pressure gauge level was dropping quickly. "This ain't happenin'!" Ronny exclaimed under his breath.

"We blew a hydraulic hose. Better call maintenance," Ronny called down out of Buddy's cab, forlornly.

Scott just shook his head repeatedly as he got out his phone and jumped in his truck to get out of the rain. Sam was concerned about Buddy. Could he be fixed?

"Is the backhoe broken?" Sam asked Ronny.

"It sure looks that way, Boss," Ronny replied, jumping out of Buddy's cab down to the ground. The rain soaked him almost immediately as he walked over to the trench.

"You got that pig ready?" Luis asked Scott as he just finished digging.

"What's a pig?" Sam asked.

"Oh, it's a big pink hairy thing that makes this noise: oink, oink, oink!" snorted Ronny.

Some of the guys chuckled and Sam laughed too.

"Naw, a pig is a device we use to clear out a tunnel so that we can make sure the new tubes get where they need to be. The pig clears out any dirt obstructions when we have a long tube like this one here," Ronny explained. "It helps the job go faster. You know, more efficiently."

The guys helped Luis load the pig down in the trench. Father Time went down to the end of the intersection to wait for the pig to get through the trench to the other side. Luis explained that the pig had sensors on it so that they could track its progress to see how far down in the tunnel it was going. Sam thought to himself, "This is the kind of thing I would like to invent someday."

Scott came back in his truck and stopped it with a screech. He and Ronny were talking back at the trench by Buddy. Ronny started waving his arms around and talking loudly. Scott was yelling loudly back at Ronny. Sam had never seen them argue before, so he watched, confused and not knowing what to expect. The argument went on. Ronny was complaining about the long—very long—hours they were spending at night on this job.

"We are going to be here all night at the rate we're goin!" Ronny complained.

"If you would get to helpin' instead of complainin', maybe we could go faster," Scott retorted.

"What am I supposed to do about it?" Ronny yelled back.

Then Scott did something strange. He took off his hard hat and threw it on the ground as hard as he could and then held his arms out at his sides with an exasperated look on his face.

Sam had seen his Mom, an avid hockey fan, do something similar while watching a hockey game on TV.

Both Ronny and Scott both walked away in frustration.

"Are they mad at each other?" Sam asked Luis.

"It looks that way. Sometimes a job gets tough. Folks lose their patience. I am sure they will work it out when they cool down," Luis said.

All the crew kept working, looking straight down, as if nothing had happened.

"That's Ronny for ya," Luis said, looking up from the trench. "He can be a hothead sometimes. Scott don't mean nothin' by it. It's just tough with all these different lines down here." Luis seemed cool under pressure. Nothing seemed to get to him.

Sam reached in to his vest pocket to find his notepad. He flipped to the page that had "Sam's Levers for Leaders" on it. He read through it, feeling bad that the crew had argued. He got out his pencil and added a sixth lever to the bottom of the list.

Sam's Levers for Leaders
1. Do the job correctly and safely.
2. Solve problems.
3. Work as a team—it's the only way!
4. Keep calm.
5. Be kind.
6. Talk about problems and stay friends.

"Time to head home," thought Sam. The party atmosphere under the tent was gone.

8

BUDDY ON THE MEND

By the afternoon that same day, the thunderstorms and lightning caused the Fortney Construction crew to call it a day. It was unsafe for them to work during the lightning, so they packed up their supply truck and drove away for home. It was unlike them to stop working before five o'clock in the evening, but the lightning and thunder made it impossible to work past three. Sam was disappointed because when Fortney Construction finished early, he didn't get to ride around at the end of the day with Ronny and Buddy.

By afternoon the next day, the storm stopped. Sam and his backyard crew of neighborhood friends were in the middle of a construction site trench they made in the mud running along a garden in the backyard. He led the team, including Dougie, a fifth grader who was also fixated on construction, and Lauren who loved to work on Sam's backyard construction crews. Together, they dug a deep trench in his the mud by the garden and his sisters' sandbox using Dad's shovels and Sam's mini excavator that he could sit on. It had control levers just like the real thing and could dig with its bucket when he pulled the levers back and forth. He continued the trench out of the sandbox and into the backyard with a shovel. The ground was easy to shovel once he got under the grass. His plan was to lay a long piece of yellow pipe Scott had given him that was a scrap from the jobsite. He wondered how Mom and Dad would feel about him digging up the yard.

All during this "job" that they created, he couldn't help but think about poor, broken-down Buddy. Was he fixed and back on the job?

"Did you see Fortney Construction today?" Sam asked Dougie while he lined up four construction cones around the grass. Dougie was a regular at the jobsite too.

"No. Spanish class." Dougie shook his head, panting in response as he hauled the large piece of heavy, yellow pipe closer to the trench.

"The backhoe is broken-down. Did you know that?"

"No, it's fixed. I saw it before we came here." Dougie was an authority on backhoes and anything construction. He had a whole room in his house full of wires, tools, pipes, hard hats, and anything construction-related. He used these materials to build model construction jobs in this spare room at his house.

What Dougie said next dropped like a bomb inside Sam's head. "The job at the intersection of Academy and Beaver was the last part of the job for Fortney Construction." Sam didn't want to think about this. He remembered the borough manager, Mr. O'Hara, telling him that the intersection at Academy and Beaver was the end of the job. He told Sam that after Fortney Construction's work was done, the roads would be milled and paved through the fall and that more big equipment would be coming. But this was little consolation to Sam. What would he do without Fortney Construction? Would he see Scott and the crew again? What about Buddy? He was troubled and saddened by the thought of the job ending. Sam stared ahead, deep in thought. A single, bright yellow maple leaf, with all its beautiful pointed edges, floated lightly and slowly down from the sky, landing at Sam's feet. Another reminder that the beginning of school and the end of Fortney Construction were near.

Lauren picked up several pieces of black corrugated pipe that Sam's mom had gotten him at the hardware store. "Where do these go?"

"Uh, right here in the hole," Sam said, snapping back to reality. "See if they can connect to the yellow pipe," he instructed. He was playing the role of the foreman on the job. The day before, Lauren had been the foreman. It was only fair to rotate the job because everyone liked it the best.

"Copy that," Lauren said into the walkie-talkie they used in the backyard jobsite even though Sam was only standing a few feet away.

They were making good progress on their sand and mud dig when Dougie announced it was time to go for dinner. Lauren had to head off to soccer practice.

Sam protested loudly, "But, guys, the job isn't done."

"See you later, Lauren. Bye, Dougie. We can finish tomorrow. Come back tomorrow, okay?" All of the sudden it was okay that they had to go home for dinner.

Sam raced down Beaver Street toward the jobsite with his dad following behind him. The crew was still toiling at the intersection of Academy and Beaver Streets. They had finished the trenching and were working on the hook up. The whole area smelled awful and sour like gas.

"Stand upwind." Scott motioned to Sam's dad, waving his arm. "Gas leak today. Lots of old lines down there and we hit one of 'em." He had to shout over the loud hum of the generator. Several strips of shriveled, rusted brown pipe lay on the street. A thin metal plate and a ladder were in the trench to keep it from caving in.

Sam waved to Diana, the flagger, as he ran toward Buddy, who was getting ready for the backfilling with a bucket of sand, idling near the trench.

"Stand where you want the sand," Ronny yelled out from Buddy's cab.

Luis waved Ronny onto where the sand was needed and held up his closed fist for the "stop" signal.

"Hey, Boss!" Ronny said, waving to Sam.

Sam waved back.

"Buddy, you're back! You're all better!" Sam thought to himself, running breathlessly up to the backhoe.

"Just a few busted hoses. Nothin' difficult for maintenance to fix. They came with the parts I needed and, presto, good as new," he imagined Buddy said through a series of loud screeches and clanks.

"Wow, good as new! Ronny, can I ride with you to dump the sand and get more from the yard?" Sam called up to Ronny in the cab, shading his eyes from the hot evening sun.

"Sure, hop in." Ronny knew that Sam had been missing these rides over the last few days.

The cab felt wonderfully cool. Sam wiped his head under his hard hat. He was sweating from all his backyard excavation.

"It doesn't smell like gas in here!" Sam announced and Ronny laughed.

"Yeah, we hit a gas line and there's a pretty major leak out there. But 'ol Johnny is helping us get it fixed," Ronny replied, pointing to Mr. Johnson. Sam waved. Mr. Johnson waved back and then climbed down in the trench for a better look.

"How did Buddy get fixed, Ronny?" Sam asked.

"Maintenance came out and fixed it quick. Pretty messy work," Ronny replied.

"The hydraulic units are connected to steel tubes and rubber hoses. Oil leaked through these hoses, making it necessary to replace them. It was a dirty job.

"It was obvious that the hose had burst by looking at the pressure gauge, which was a lot lower than it was supposed to be. That broken hose spilled a large amount of oil in a short time, so it was easy to find the leak," Ronny explained.

"Then, the mechanics figure out if the hydraulic unit the hose serves is active. The oil in an active unit is under pressure and it could explode if it's not loosened the right way. That can cause a huge, oily mess. You have to have a bucket ready for that," Ronny continued.

Sam imagined Buddy was explaining the maintenance steps like someone would explain their recent medical surgery. "Want to hear what they do next? They remove the fittings on each end of the hose with a wrench. ...d when the wrenches loosen pieces in my ...ics. I tell you, it's like loosening your belt. It's also important not to damage an O-ring while turning the wrenches. A damaged O ring can cause a leak." Sam laughed to himself at this picture in his mind.

Sam held the steering wheel tightly. He thought about the end of the job. He wanted to ask Ronny what would happen when this job was over. He wanted to ask, but he couldn't. He felt a weird feeling in his throat, like he couldn't swallow. He didn't want to get teary in front of Ronny, so he decided just to enjoy the ride.

Ronny dumped the sand and was moving levers and the steering wheel all at the same time. He turned Buddy around and they whizzed down Beaver Street toward the yard, bumping and roaring. Ronny let Sam steer

Buddy down Beaver the short distance to the yard. Sam saw Dougie's dad driving by. He did a double take when he recognized it was Sam at the wheel of the backhoe. Sam waved eagerly. He was having the time of his life.

9

SCHOOL STARTS

"Mom, will I be any good at school this year?" Sam asked as he headed toward the school for his first day back. He was excited to be going back to school in some ways. His friends would be there and they could play four square, run down, or punt the football at recess. But at the same time, he would miss the completion of the work at the jobsite, and that annoyed him. He had heard his new teacher would be fun. But what if she was boring? And what if he couldn't read well enough? He was sure he hadn't memorized all of his multiplication tables. The beginning of the school year always seemed a bit overwhelming to Sam.

"You will be great at school. You are very smart and ask good questions. As long as you be yourself, listen to the teacher, and do your best, it will all be fine." Mom stood on the sidewalk looking at Sam with certainty. "You will love your class once you get to know the routine. And, you know a couple of the kids in the class already. Your teacher, Miss Matthews, wore a 'Thing One' costume from *The Cat in the Hat* at Halloween last year with a huge blue furry wig. Anyone that does that must be fun!"

Sam wasn't so sure. It had been a great summer. He thought about all the fun he had watching Fortney Construction from the very first day. Not only was he getting less time to watch the jobsite, the job was almost over and he was going to be missing it.

"I don't want to go to school today. I just want to go to the Fortney Construction jobsite and watch construction," Sam announced.

Sam then remembered what Scott, Ronny, and Luis each said to get an education. He remembered that Scott said that he would need to be smart to run a backhoe. That he needed to be able to do math, measure, and use a computer. Sam remembered his words very clearly. "If you want to learn construction, engineering, and excavating, you have to learn how to read and do math." He realized that all of the Fortney Construction crew started by going to school. He needed to go to school, too.

"But I already know how to read, add, and subtract," Sam thought to himself, defiantly.

"But how would I read one of those big manuals? Could I run a backhoe, design a building, or be the foreman of a crew? How would I figure out how many crewmembers I needed? How would I figure out how big your building should be?" These were all questions he asked himself.

"I better stick with school for now," he told himself.

"But, what happens when Fortney Construction is done with this job? Will I ever see Scott again? What will they do with the backhoe?" Sam's emotions were building like Buddy's pressure gauges. He was unsure, confused, sad, and excited all at the same time. He wasn't sure he wanted a new routine. He liked the routine with Fortney Construction.

He knew Scott and the crew would go on to new jobs, maybe somewhere close by or maybe in another state. He knew Scott wanted to get back to Kentucky where he was from so that he could be close to his family again. Sam wanted him to be happy.

"I will try to stay in touch with Scott, Ronny, Luis, and the team somehow," thought Sam. "Construction jobs don't last forever but there are always more jobs to watch. It's hard to think about them moving on to another job and I sure will miss them. But I still have a few more days to watch them after school. Right now, I need to focus on doing well at school. That is my job right now," Sam told himself. And he felt better.

Sam remembered what his mom said to him earlier in the summer, "You know, Sam, you have a lot of potential to do great things with your life."

Sam felt a wave of accomplishment wash over him. Spending time learning construction that summer had been a good thing. He had learned a lot watching a dedicated team of hard-working people complete a complicated job had been quite an education. He had done things that no other kid he knew had done.

He thought about all that he had learned that summer as he walked up to the school. Kids with backpacks were swarming toward the school from all directions.

"What am I supposed to be? What will I be doing in the future? I know I want to do something with construction, but how do I get there?" he wondered.

Then, it hit him. He could tie the two together, of course! He would figure out how to make school projects fit his interests. He knew there would be plenty of school projects and book reports ahead that could be construction or building related.

That day after school, Sam burst in the back door, swinging his backpack off and grinning ear to ear.

"This year IS going to be fun!" he yelled out to Mom. He hopped on the computer to search for more big machine videos. One of them would be perfect to help with his first report due by the end of the month.

After several searches on the computer, Sam left home and arrived at the site just in time to see the crew coordinate another large tie in. They had cut many pieces of pipe and were just lifting a super long piece of pipe onto their shoulders to carry it to the trench. It was the length of eight crewmembers with space in between each one. It took all eight crewmembers to lift the pipe; it was so heavy. They were shouting commands to each other as they struggled to get the heavy pipe to the trench. Then, they set it down gently on the ground. Sam pumped his fists into the air when they got the pipe safely on the ground.

Fortney Construction was on a deadline to get the job finished by the end of the next day. Scott said that even with the overtime the crew had worked that summer, the job was still considered profitable. Sam didn't know what that meant. Whatever it was, it was important to Scott because he had mentioned it several times that summer.

"What do you mean by 'profitable'?" Sam asked Scott.

"Oh, that's just some math that tells you if you are making money on top of what it costs to do the job. It's how the company knows if I am doin' a good job or not. It's what the big Bosses want to see."

"How many big Bosses are there?" Sam asked.

"Lots," responded Scott. "That's what you are going to be one day." He pointed a finger at Sam.

Sam was hoping he would at least get to ride in Buddy just one more time. "Do you think I could please, please ride in the backhoe one more time, especially because it's the last day?"

"Ride? You want a ride? What you want a ride for when you could operate it all by yourself?" Scott asked with one hand on his hip, head cocked to one side.

"Operate?" Sam whispered the word. He had never dreamed he would be able to *operate* Buddy by *himself*.

"Sure. You come back right before quittin' time, and we'll put you up in that cab by yourself and see how much trouble you can cause." Scott said, winking at Sam.

Sam barely ate his dinner. He was too excited to eat or do anything else except look out the window to watch for Scott's truck or a Fortney Construction vehicle riding down the street. He must have asked Mom a hundred times what time it was and if it was close to quitting time. Mom was getting a bit exasperated and was looking forward to quitting time herself.

After dinner, Sam raced to the yard. He wanted to make sure they hadn't already left. He ran up to Scott and the crew as they were finishing the paperwork on the job for the day.

"I'm ready to operate the backhoe!" Sam exclaimed.

"Main man, how are you? You ready? Okay then, hop up there, and let's see how you do. Don't go diggin' no trenches, you understand? The rules are that you can move the bucket, but don't go too deep. And, no touching the pedals," Scott instructed.

Sam's heart was beating a mile a minute.

"You can't hurt nothin' 'cause the motor's on idle," Scott said.

Sam grabbed Buddy's steering wheel.

"Are you ready for this?" he asked himself.

"Wooo-hooo!" Sam yelled as he pulled Buddy's levers, lifting the boom and bucket high in the air. Sam pulled his right hand in and moved the bucket around.

"Look at me! I'm operating the backhoe by myself!" Sam yelled in the cab, face lit up with glee. Ronny gave the thumbs up sign from the grass below.

The bucket landed down on the grass with a loud clank.

"Ooops," Sam said. "I guess I didn't go slowly enough. Sorry, Buddy. Did that hurt?" Sam asked out loud.

"It's so easy to work the levers!" Sam yelled again.

A neighbor friend who worked for a big manufacturing company in town stopped by, watching Sam at the controls.

"Was that you I saw flagging at the intersection of Pine and Beaver a few weeks ago?" the neighbor yelled up to Sam.

Sam nodded.

"And was that you shoveling a few days ago down there at Academy?"

"Yes, I am at the jobsite a lot. It's sort of my main interest these days."

"Yes, I can tell. You should stick with that interest. Then you can come and work for me at my company someday."

"Great. I am available for work now if you need some extra help." Sam suggested, hoping to find another crew to work with.

The man smiled and said, "I will keep that in mind. I believe you would be a big asset to my company someday."

Together, Sam and Buddy continued to move levers, swivel around from the front seat to the backseat, and generally pushed every button that Buddy had for over an hour.

"I love to pllaayyy!" Sam imagined Buddy bellowing.

Wild horses could not have pulled Sam out of Buddy's cab. It was starting to get dark, however, and Sam knew his time was coming close to an end.

"Buddy, will I ever see you again?" Sam's eyes were full of tears. "Where are you going next?" Sam wondered.

"I don't know, but wherever it is, I hope you are there," he imagined Buddy responding.

Sam wondered if he would ever be as happy again as he was right then.

Then, as if Buddy was talking to him directly, Sam made up his mind that he would have many more construction experiences. He had a feeling that he was headed for great things in the construction and building field. This was his dream, his calling.

He imagined Buddy saying, "Be the person you are meant to be, Sam. Follow your dreams about construction and start now, while you are in school. Don't wait. After all, you are the Construction Kid. Be the person you are meant to be. Be the foreman of the class."

11

SAYING GOODBYE

"It's the last day for Fortney Construction, Dad," Sam said sadly, as Dad left for work.

"Well, you've had a great time with them and have learned a lot. Tell them I said 'bye' and thank them for all the times they let you drive down Beaver Street in the backhoe. Can you believe you got to do that?"

Sam and Dad laughed, thinking about how crazy fantastic it was that Sam was able to drive a backhoe.

"And operate it!" Sam added. "For my birthday, can we rent a packer?"

"What? Are you kidding? Where would we use that?" Dad actually loved this "out of the box" thinking.

"In the yard," Sam replied, certain of himself and the idea.

"No way, dude. Have fun and see you later." Dad pulled the door shut and left for work.

Sam wore his Fortney Construction T-shirt to school that day. It was very hot that day after school. Fortney Construction was coasting on that last day, just backfilling the last deep trench most of the day. No more tough decisions to make, given that the job was essentially done. Sam arrived at the jobsite in his Fortney Construction T-shirt, hard hat, orange vest, and snow boots. They were the closest thing he had to steel toed shoes. Dougie was there, too. He was sitting near the trench in the small spot of shade in the area. This was the last day with his crew.

Sam stood by the trench, watching Buddy, Skids, and the dump truck completing the backfilling routine. First, they dumped loads of sand in the trench and Alex, Luis, Ronny, and the others smoothed the sand out with their shovels. Because the trench at this intersection was so huge, spanning the length of the intersection and extending well into the roads at each of the four points, the sand filling alone took hours.

Sam was sweating and red faced. He refused to stand in the shade. He felt it was important to stand as near the work as he could. He wanted to soak in every minute of the Fortney Construction crew, the vehicles, and what they did best. He felt at *his* best when he was there by the trench watching and helping.

Sam asked if he could help spread out the dirt and "buff up" or clean up the dirt that fell on the road outside the trench. Luis said sure. He was in charge when Scott was not on the jobsite. Luis was going to his next job as the foreman of the job. Scott had explained to Sam that it was due to Luis' knowledge and hard work that he was able to become a foreman. Sam really liked Luis and wanted to be just like him, Scott, and Ronny. He really looked up to each of them.

It was time for the final stage of the backfilling. Sam loved the smell of the coal patch and, without asking, positioned himself right next to the crew when Buddy slowly dumped the oozing coal patch down on top of the dirt, providing the final covering to the hole. No more trench. Sam smoothed the coal patch around, following Ronny's instructions on how to best use the shovel and where to put the coal patch.

Mr. O'Hara stopped by the jobsite to check Fortney Construction's progress. Because it was the last day, he wanted to make sure the job was being finished properly. He saw Sam and Dougie, the devoted construction followers.

"Sam, I believe you have logged in as many hours as anyone on the crew on this job," he said, patting Sam on the back. "You are one of the most devoted, hardworking guys I have ever seen. I am going to put you on the payroll. How would you like to work for me?"

"Sure!" said Sam, beaming. "But I have to finish my work on this job first."

Mr. O'Hara, Ronny, Alex, Luis, and Scott all laughed.

"Well, don't you worry," said Mr. O'Hara. "There is plenty of road milling and paving yet to come. All of these roads with these Fortney Construction patches are going to be resurfaced and the sidewalks replaced. That's the next construction job that's coming, complete with huge milling machines and the whole nine yards. It's a big job, and we will need you to make sure it's done right." He waved and crossed the road to go back to his car.

Alex turned to Sam and said, "Sam, I believe you are going to be my boss someday."

Sam replied with a smile, "I thought I was the boss now."

More laughter from everyone.

The job was winding down. All the backfilling and patching were done. The crew was picking up the cones and signs. The flaggers had gone home. The constant roaring of the equipment was gone, leaving a fresh silence in its place. Scott said he was heading back to Kentucky and had to fill his truck up with gas for the long ride.

"I guess I better clean out this 'ol truck somewhere between here and Kentucky before my wife sees what a mess I have made in here." Scott and Sam laughed. Sam knew the final moments of seeing Scott and enjoying his bright, warm, and generous personality were coming.

Sam decided to seize the opportunity to thank the crew. Scott, Ronny, and Alex were standing close by.

"Scott, I wanted to thank you and all the guys for helping me learn so much this summer. I think what I have learned will really help me be a backhoe man someday." He was glad he was able to get that out without tearing up, but he felt like tearing up just the same.

Ronny said, "I'll never forget you, Construction Kid. You made my job a lot easier. Be good and work hard in school, you hear?"

Sam stood absolutely still and stared down at the ground. He didn't say a word, which was unusual for him. He thought hard so that he could hold onto this memory for a long time, just like the photo would be imbedded in a camera. Without being prompted, Sam offered his tiny hand to Ronny, Scott, Luis, and Alex. He shook each of their giant hands in turn. All he said was, "Thank you." He was trying his best not to cry in front of the crew.

Sam walked slowly by Buddy, who was parked on the side of the road, his hand running alongside of Buddy's body. He patted Buddy's boom.

"Bye. I promise I will see you sometime," Sam whispered.

Walking back home from the jobsite for the last time, he looked at the patches on the road all along Beaver Street. He thought they would be like souvenirs from the work, from the summer. Every time he would look at them, he decided, they would be warm reminders of the best summer of his life.

As he walked home, Sam decided that moving on to the next fun thing can mean leaving the last fun thing behind, but not for good, not completely. He decided that if he remembered all the good times he had and the lessons he learned, the crew would still be close to him any time he wanted them to be.

Sam knew in his heart he would always remember Fortney Construction and what they had taught him. This job was only the beginning. He would work on a crew again...and it would be just as extraordinary. Maybe even more.

FINAL THOUGHTS

G.G. Webb

It was really fun to be with the crew. They helped me learn a lot more about construction and let me experience a lot more of construction. Mainly, I just like technology. My favorite part of that summer was going in the backhoes because they were fun to operate. To actually get more detail as to what a backhoe is and experience the jobs it does was a great experience for me. Mini excavators are also fun because they are small and can do jobs when larger excavators can't fit in tight spaces. My second favorite machine is the packer because it goes up and down, pressuring things down, which is neat.

Kids love construction so much because it's inspiring. The machines look amazing and can do so many unique things. They are so powerful, it's almost unbelievable. I hope other kids like this book.

Things to buy at the hardware store for backyard construction projects:

1. Short lengths of corrugated pipe
2. Roll of caution tape
3. Electrical tape
4. Tape measure
5. Level
6. Hard hat
7. Plastic toolbox
8. Protective gloves and face masks
9. Construction signs
10. Plastic fencing to put around the jobsite
11. Hand tools for digging, smoothing, and flattening
12. Bolts, screws, and plastic fittings

Backyard Construction Project Ideas

1. Bury pieces of corrugated pipe in your gravel driveway, garden, or sandbox. Fill the pipes with rocks, sand, water, a garden hose, or whatever you have to see how they travel through the pipe.

2. Bury the pieces of corrugated pipe in the snow—if you live where it snows. It's great fun to create tunnels and easy to dig under the snow.

3. Make a construction snowman using a hard hat, vest, gloves, and a piece of pipe instead of a broom in the hands.

4. Use the underside of a play set or tree house as a jobsite to do repairs or maintenance. Pretend you are fixing the underside of a backhoe or building, attaching pipes with tape.

5. Create an equipment rental shop. Pretend to rent toys, bikes, shovels, etc. Use paper on a clipboard to write down each item for rent, how much the rental fees are, and when the item must be returned.

Made in the USA
Lexington, KY
06 August 2015